Pope Benedict XVI

BEHOLD THE LAMB OF GOD

REFLECTIONS ON THE EUCHARIST

*Extracts from his writings and speeches
selected by Fr Gerard Skinner*

FAMILY PUBLICATIONS

Papal Texts © Libreria Editrice Vaticana 2005-09
Design © Family Publications 2010
Cover Image © Stefano Spaziani 2009

ISBN 978 1 907380 02 0

published by

Family Publications
Denis Riches House, 66 Sandford Lane
Kennington, Oxford OX1 5RP
www.familypublications.co.uk

Printed by Cromwell Press Group,
Trowbridge, Wilts.

Contents

Introduction

Late on an autumn afternoon towards the end of 2005 – the Year of the Eucharist that had been inaugurated by Pope John Paul II – Pope Benedict XVI met a large group of children who had that year made their First Holy Communion. He recalled the day of his own First Holy Communion saying that

> at the heart of my joyful and beautiful memories is this one . . . I understood that Jesus had entered my heart, he had actually visited me. And with Jesus, God himself was with me. And I realized that this is a gift of love that is truly worth more than all the other things that life can give. So on that day I was really filled with great joy, because Jesus came to me and I realized that a new stage in my life was beginning, I was nine years old, and that it was henceforth important to stay faithful to that encounter, to that communion. I promised the Lord as best I could: "I always want to stay with you," and I prayed to him, "but above all, stay with me." So I went on living my life like that; thanks be to God, the Lord has always taken me by the hand and guided me, even in difficult situations.

One of the children asked how Jesus could be present in the Eucharist, and yet remain unseen. As the lights of St Peter's Square came on, Pope Benedict spoke of some of the many things that we cannot see but yet exist and are essential, including electricity that shows its presence in diverse ways including light:

> So it is with the Risen Lord: we do not see him with our eyes but we see that wherever Jesus is, people change, they improve. A greater capacity for peace, for reconciliation, etc., is created. Therefore, we do not see the Lord himself but we see the effects of the Lord: so we can understand that Jesus is present . . . it is precisely the invisible things that are the most profound, the most important. So let us go to meet this invisible but powerful Lord who helps us to live well.

In speaking to the children the Holy Father was simply retelling his lifetime's understanding and devotion to the Eucharistic Presence of Christ. In the following pages we hear Pope Benedict doing the same as he contemplates the Sacrament of Sacraments, the veiled Real Presence of the Risen Lord, and we hear him say, in words similar to these with which he addressed the children of Rome,

"Jesus, I am yours. I will follow you in my life, I never want to lose this friendship, this communion with you. . . I am yours, and I ask you, please stay with me always."

Fr Gerard Skinner
London, Feast of Ss Simon & Jude, 2009

I
HOMILIES

MASS AND EUCHARISTIC PROCESSION ON THE SOLEMNITY OF CORPUS DOMINI

Square in front of the Basilica of St John Lateran
Thursday, 26 May 2005

'We Walk with the Risen One'

On the feast of Corpus Domini, the Church relives the mystery of Holy Thursday in the light of the Resurrection. There is also a Eucharistic procession on Holy Thursday, when the Church repeats the exodus of Jesus from the Upper Room to the Mount of Olives.

In Israel, the night of the Passover was celebrated in the home, within the intimacy of the family; this is how the first Passover in Egypt was commemorated, the night in which the blood of the paschal lamb, sprinkled on the crossbeam and doorposts of the houses, served as protection against the destroyer.

On that night, Jesus goes out and hands himself over to the betrayer, the destroyer, and in so doing, overcomes the night, overcomes the darkness of evil. Only in this way is the gift of the Eucharist, instituted in the Upper Room, fulfilled: Jesus truly gives his Body and his Blood. Crossing over the threshold of death, he becomes living Bread, true manna, endless nourishment for eternity. The flesh becomes the Bread of Life.

In the Holy Thursday procession, the Church accompanies

Jesus to the Mount of Olives: it is the authentic desire of the Church in prayer to keep watch with Jesus, not to abandon him in the night of the world, on the night of betrayal, on the night of the indifference of many people.

On the feast of Corpus Domini, we again go on this procession, but in the joy of the Resurrection. The Lord is risen and leads us. In the narrations of the Resurrection there is a common and essential feature; the angels say: the Lord "goes ahead of you to Galilee, where you will see him" (Mt 28: 7).

Taking this into deep consideration, we can say that this "going ahead" of Jesus implies a two-way direction.

The first is, as we have heard, Galilee. In Israel, Galilee was considered to be the doorway to the pagan world. And in reality, precisely on the mountain in Galilee, the disciples see Jesus, the Lord, who tells them: "Go . . . and make disciples of all the nations" (Mt 28: 19).

The other preceding direction of the Risen One appears in the Gospel of St John, in the words of Jesus to Mary Magdalene: "Do not hold me, for I have not yet ascended to the Father" (Jn 20: 17).

Jesus goes before us next to the Father, rises to the heights of God and invites us to follow him. These two directions on the Risen One's journey are not contradictory, for both indicate the path to follow Christ.

The true purpose of our journey is communion with God. He himself is the house of many dwelling places (cf. Jn 14: 2ff.); but we can be elevated to these dwelling places only by going "towards Galilee", travelling on the pathways of the world, taking the Gospel to all nations, carrying the gift of his love to the men and women of all times.

Therefore, the journey of the Apostles extends to the "ends of the earth" (cf. Acts 1: 6ff.). In this way, Sts Peter and Paul went all the way to Rome, a city that at that time was the centre of the known world, the true *caput mundi.*

The Holy Thursday procession accompanies Jesus in his solitude towards the *via crucis.* The Corpus Domini procession responds instead in a symbolic way to the mandate of the Risen One: I go before you to Galilee. Go to the extreme ends of the world, take the Gospel to the world.

Of course, by faith, the Eucharist is an intimate mystery. The Lord instituted the Sacrament in the Upper Room, surrounded by his new family, by the twelve Apostles, a prefiguration and anticipation of the Church of all times.

And so, in the liturgy of the ancient Church, the distribution of Holy Communion was introduced with the words *Sancta sanctis*: the holy gift is intended for those who have been made holy.

In this way a response was given to the exhortation of St Paul to the Corinthians: "A man should examine himself first; only then should he eat of the bread and drink of the cup . . ." (I Cor 11: 28).

Nevertheless, from this intimacy that is a most personal gift of the Lord, the strength of the Sacrament of the Eucharist goes above and beyond the walls of our churches. In this Sacrament, the Lord is always journeying to meet the world. This universal aspect of the Eucharistic presence becomes evident in today's festive procession.

We bring Christ, present under the sign of bread, onto the streets of our city. We entrust these streets, these homes, our daily life, to his goodness. May our streets be streets of Jesus! May our houses be homes for him and with him! May our life of every day be penetrated by his presence.

With this gesture, let us place under his eyes the sufferings of the sick, the solitude of young people and the elderly, temptations, fears – our entire life. The procession represents an immense and public blessing for our city: Christ is, in person, the divine Blessing for the world. May the ray of his blessing extend to us all!

In the Corpus Domini procession, we walk with the Risen One on his journey to meet the entire world, as we said. By doing precisely this, we too answer his mandate: "Take, eat . . . Drink of it, all of you" (Mt 26: 26ff.).

It is not possible to "eat" the Risen One, present under the sign of bread, as if it were a simple piece of bread. To eat this Bread is to communicate, to enter into communion with the person of the living Lord. This communion, this act of "eating", is truly an encounter between two persons, it is allowing our lives to be penetrated by the life of the One who is the Lord, of the One who is my Creator and Redeemer.

The purpose of this communion, of this partaking, is the assimilation of my life with his, my transformation and conformation into he who is living Love. Therefore, this communion implies adoration, it implies the will to follow Christ, to follow the One who goes ahead of us. Adoration and procession thereby make up a single gesture of communion; they answer his mandate: "Take and eat".

Our procession finishes in front of the Basilica of St Mary Major in the encounter with Our Lady, called by the dear Pope John Paul II, "Woman of the Eucharist". Mary, Mother of the Lord, truly teaches us what entering into communion with Christ is: Mary offered her own flesh, her own blood to Jesus and became a living tent of the Word, allowing herself to be penetrated by his presence in body and spirit.

Let us pray to her, our holy Mother, so that she may help us to open our entire being, always more, to Christ's presence; so that she may help us to follow him faithfully, day after day, on the streets of our life. Amen.

From the Homily given during the

PASTORAL VISIT OF HIS HOLINESS BENEDICT XVI TO BARI FOR THE CLOSING OF THE 24th ITALIAN NATIONAL EUCHARISTIC CONGRESS

Esplanade of Marisabella
Sunday, 29 May 2005

'Glorify the Lord, Jerusalem; Zion, praise your God'

The invitation of the Psalmist that is also echoed in the Sequence expresses very clearly the meaning of this Eucharistic Celebration: we are gathered here to praise and bless the Lord. This is what urged the Italian Church to gather here in Bari on the occasion of the National Eucharistic Congress.

I also wanted to join all of you today to give special emphasis to the celebration of the Solemnity of the Body and Blood of Christ, thus to pay homage to Christ in the Sacrament of his love and at the same time to strengthen the bonds of communion that bind me to the Church in Italy and to her Pastors. My venerable and beloved Predecessor, Pope John Paul II, would also have liked to have been here at this important ecclesial event, as you know. We all feel that he is close to us and with us is glorifying Christ, the Good Shepherd, whom he can now contemplate directly. . . .

The intention of this Eucharistic Congress, which ends today, was once again to present Sunday as the "weekly Easter", an expression of the identity of the Christian community and the centre of its life and mission.

The chosen theme – *"Without Sunday we cannot live"* – takes us back to the year 304, when the Emperor Diocletian forbade Christians, on pain of death, from possessing the Scriptures, from gathering on Sundays to celebrate the Eucharist, and from building places in which to hold their assemblies.

In Abitene, a small village in present-day Tunisia, 49 Christians were taken by surprise one Sunday while they were celebrating the Eucharist, gathered in the house of Octavius Felix, thereby defying the imperial prohibitions. They were arrested and taken to Carthage to be interrogated by the Proconsul Anulinus.

Significant among other things is the answer a certain Emeritus gave to the Proconsul who asked him why on earth they had disobeyed the Emperor's severe orders. He replied: *"Sine dominico non possumus"*: that is, we cannot live without joining together on Sunday to celebrate the Eucharist. We would lack the strength to face our daily problems and not to succumb.

After atrocious tortures, these 49 martyrs of Abitene were killed. Thus, they confirmed their faith with bloodshed. They died, but they were victorious: today we remember them in the glory of the Risen Christ.

The experience of the martyrs of Abitene is also one on which we twenty-first-century Christians should reflect. It is not easy for us either to live as Christians, even if we are spared such prohibitions from the emperor. From a spiritual point of view, the world in which we find ourselves, often marked by unbridled consumerism, religious indifference and a secularism closed to transcendence, can appear a desert just as "vast and terrible" (Dt 8: 15) as the one we heard about in the first reading from the Book of Deuteronomy. God came to the aid of the Jewish people in difficulty in this desert with his gift of manna, to make them understand that "not by bread alone does man live, but by every word that comes forth from the mouth of the Lord" (Dt 8: 3).

In today's Gospel, Jesus has explained to us, through the gift of manna, for what bread God wanted to prepare the people of the New Covenant. Alluding to the Eucharist he said: "This is the bread that came down from heaven. Unlike your ancestors who ate and died nonetheless, the man who feeds on this bread shall live forever" (Jn 6: 58).

In taking flesh, the Son of God could become Bread and thus be the nourishment of his people, of us, journeying on in this world towards the promised land of Heaven.

We need this Bread to face the fatigue and weariness of our journey. Sunday, the Lord's Day, is a favourable opportunity to draw strength from him, the Lord of life.

The Sunday precept is not, therefore, an externally imposed duty, a burden on our shoulders. On the contrary, taking part in the Celebration, being nourished by the Eucharistic Bread and experiencing the communion of their brothers and sisters in Christ is a need for Christians, it is a joy; Christians can thus replenish the energy they need to continue on the journey we must make every week.

Moreover, this is not an arbitrary journey: the path God points out to us through his Word goes in the direction inscribed in man's very existence. The Word of God and reason go together. For the human being, following the Word of God, going with Christ means fulfilling oneself; losing it is equivalent to losing oneself.

The Lord does not leave us alone on this journey. He is with us; indeed, he wishes to share our destiny to the point of identifying with us.

In the Gospel discourse that we have just heard he says, "He who feeds on my flesh and drinks my blood remains in me, and

I in him" (Jn 6: 56). How is it possible not to rejoice in such a promise?

However, we have heard that at his first announcement, instead of rejoicing, the people started to murmur in protest: "How can he give us his flesh to eat?" (Jn 6: 52). To tell the truth, that attitude has frequently been repeated in the course of history. One might say that basically people do not want to have God so close, to be so easily within reach or to share so deeply in the events of their daily life.

Rather, people want him to be great and, in brief, we also often want him to be a little distant from us. Questions are then raised that are intended to show that, after all, such closeness would be impossible.

But the words that Christ spoke on that occasion have lost none of their clarity: "Let me solemnly assure you, if you do not eat the flesh of the Son of Man and drink his blood, you have no life in you" (Jn 6: 53). Truly, we need a God who is close to us. In the face of the murmur of protest, Jesus might have fallen back on reassuring words: "Friends", he could have said, "do not worry! I spoke of flesh but it is only a symbol. What I mean is only a deep communion of sentiments."

But no, Jesus did not have recourse to such soothing words. He stuck to his assertion, to all his realism, even when he saw many of his disciples breaking away (cf. Jn 6: 66). Indeed, he showed his readiness to accept even desertion by his apostles, while not in any way changing the substance of his discourse: "Do you want to leave me too?" (Jn 6: 67), he asked. Thanks be to God, Peter's response was one that even we can make our own today with full awareness: "Lord, to whom shall we go? You have the words of eternal life" (Jn 6: 68). We need a God who is close, a God who puts himself in our hands and who loves us.

Christ is truly present among us in the Eucharist. His presence is not static. It is a dynamic presence that grasps us, to make us his own, to make us assimilate him. Christ draws us to him, he makes us come out of ourselves to make us all one with him. In this way he also integrates us in the communities of brothers and sisters, and communion with the Lord is always also communion with our brothers and sisters. And we see the beauty of this communion that the Blessed Eucharist gives us.

We are touching on a further dimension of the Eucharist that I would like to point out before concluding.

The Christ whom we meet in the Sacrament is the same here in Bari as he is in Rome, here in Europe, as in America, Africa, Asia and Oceania. He is the one same Christ who is present in the Eucharistic Bread of every place on earth. This means that we can encounter him only together with all others. We can only receive him in unity.

Is not this what the Apostle Paul said in the reading we have just heard? In writing to the Corinthians he said: "Because the loaf of bread is one, we, many though we are, are one body, for we all partake of the one loaf" (I Cor 10: 17).

The consequence is clear: we cannot communicate with the Lord if we do not communicate with one another. If we want to present ourselves to him, we must also take a step towards meeting one another.

To do this we must learn the great lesson of forgiveness: we must not let the gnawings of resentment work in our soul, but must open our hearts to the magnanimity of listening to others, open our hearts to understanding them, eventually to accepting their apologies, to generously offering our own.

The Eucharist, let us repeat, is the sacrament of unity. Unfortunately, however, Christians are divided, precisely in the sacrament of unity. Sustained by the Eucharist, we must feel all the more roused to striving with all our strength for that full unity which Christ ardently desired in the Upper Room.

Precisely here in Bari, fortunate Bari, a city that preserves the bones of St Nicholas, a land of encounter and dialogue with our Christian brethren of the East, I would like to reaffirm my desire to assume as a fundamental commitment working with all my might for the re-establishment of the full and visible unity of all Christ's followers.

I am aware that expressions of good will do not suffice for this. We need concrete acts that penetrate souls and shake consciences, prompting each one to that inner conversion that is the necessary condition for any progress on the path of ecumenism.[*]

I ask you all to set out with determination on the path of that spiritual ecumenism which, through prayer, opens the doors to the Holy Spirit, who alone can create unity.

Dear friends who have come to Bari from various parts of Italy to celebrate this Eucharistic Congress, we must rediscover the joy of Christian Sundays. We must proudly rediscover the privilege of sharing in the Eucharist, which is the sacrament of the renewed world.

Christ's Resurrection happened on the first day of the week, which in the Scriptures is the day of the world's creation. For this very reason Sunday was considered by the early Christian community as the day on which the new world began, the one on which, with Christ's victory over death, the new creation began.

As they gathered round the Eucharistic table, the community was taking shape as a new people of God. St Ignatius of Antioch described Christians as "having attained new hope" and presented them as people "who lived in accordance with Sunday" ("*iuxta dominicam viventes*"). In this perspective, the Bishop of Antioch wondered: "How will we be able to live without him, the One whom the prophets so long awaited?" (*Ep. ad Magnesios,* 9, 1-2).

---

[*] Cf. Message to the Universal Church, Sistine Chapel, 20 April 2005; *L'Osservatore Romano* English Edition, 27 April, p. 3.

"How will we be able to live without him?" In these words of St Ignatius we hear echoing the affirmation of the martyrs of Abitene: "*Sine dominico non possumus*".

It is this that gives rise to our prayer: that we too, Christians of today, will rediscover an awareness of the crucial importance of the Sunday Celebration and will know how to draw from participation in the Eucharist the necessary dynamism for a new commitment to proclaiming to the world Christ "our peace" (Eph 2: 14). Amen!

HOLY MASS AND EUCHARISTIC PROCESSION ON THE SOLEMNITY OF THE SACRED BODY AND BLOOD OF CHRIST

Square in front of the Basilica of Saint John Lateran
Thursday, 15 June 2006

'The Bread of Heaven'

On the eve of his Passion, during the Passover meal, the Lord took the bread in his hands – as we heard a short time ago in the Gospel passage – and, having blessed it, he broke it and gave it to his Disciples, saying: "Take this, this is my body". He then took the chalice, gave thanks and passed it to them and they all drank from it. He said: "This is my blood, the blood of the covenant, to be poured out on behalf of many" (Mk 14: 22-24).

The entire history of God with humanity is recapitulated in these words. The past alone is not only referred to and interpreted, but the future is anticipated – the coming of the Kingdom of God into the world. What Jesus says are not simply words. What he says is an event, the central event of the history of the world and of our personal lives.

These words are inexhaustible. In this hour, I would like to meditate with you on just one aspect. Jesus, as a sign of his presence, chose bread and wine. With each one of the two signs he gives himself completely, not only in part. The Risen One is not divided. He is a person who, through signs, comes near to us and unites himself to us. Each sign however, represents in its own way a particular aspect of his mystery and through its respective manifestation, wishes to speak to us so that we learn to understand the mystery of Jesus Christ a little better.

During the procession and in adoration we look at the consecrated Host, the most simple type of bread and nourishment, made only of a little flour and water. In this way, it appears as the food of the poor, those to whom the Lord made himself closest in the first place.

The prayer with which the Church, during the liturgy of the Mass, consigns this bread to the Lord, qualifies it as fruit of the earth and the work of humans.

It involves human labour, the daily work of those who till the soil, sow and harvest [the wheat] and, finally, prepare the bread. However, bread is not purely and simply what we produce, something made by us; it is fruit of the earth and therefore is also gift.

We cannot take credit for the fact that the earth produces fruit; the Creator alone could have made it fertile. And now we too can expand a little on this prayer of the Church, saying: the bread is fruit of heaven and earth together. It implies the synergy of the forces of earth and the gifts from above, that is, of the sun and the rain. And water too, which we need to prepare the bread, cannot be produced by us.

In a period in which desertification is spoken of and where we hear time and again the warning that man and beast risk dying of thirst in these waterless regions – in such a period we realize once again how great is the gift of water and of how we are unable to produce it ourselves. And so, looking closely at this little piece of white Host, this bread of the poor appears to us as a synthesis of creation. Heaven and earth, too, like the activity and spirit of man, cooperate. The synergy of the forces that make the mystery of life and the existence of man possible on our poor planet come to meet us in all of their majestic grandeur.

In this way we begin to understand why the Lord chooses this piece of bread to represent him. Creation, with all of its gifts, aspires above and beyond itself to something even greater. Over and above the synthesis of its own forces, above and beyond the synthesis also of nature and of spirit that, in some way, we detect in the piece of bread, creation is projected towards divinization, toward the holy wedding feast, toward unification with the Creator himself.

And still, we have not yet explained in depth the message of this sign of bread. The Lord mentioned its deepest mystery on Palm Sunday, when some Greeks asked to see him. In his answer to this question is the phrase: "Truly, truly, I say to you, unless a grain of wheat falls into the earth and dies, it remains alone; but if it dies, it bears much fruit" (Jn 12: 24).

The mystery of the Passion is hidden in the bread made of ground grain. Flour, the ground wheat, presuppose the death and resurrection of the grain. In being ground and baked, it carries in itself once again the same mystery of the Passion. Only through death does resurrection arrive, as does the fruit and new life.

Mediterranean culture, in the centuries before Christ, had a profound intuition of this mystery. Based on the experience of this death and rising they created myths of divinity which, dying and rising, gave new life. To them, the cycle of nature seemed like a divine promise in the midst of the darkness of suffering and death that we are faced with. In these myths, the soul of the human person, in a certain way, reached out toward that God made man, who, humiliated unto death on a cross, in this way opened the door of life to all of us. In bread and its making, man has understood it as a waiting period of nature, like a promise of nature that this would come to exist: the God that dies and in this way brings us to life.

What was awaited in myths and that in the very grain of wheat is hidden like a sign of the hope of creation – this truly came about in Christ. Through his gratuitous suffering and death, he became bread for all of us, and with this living and certain hope. He accompanies us in all of our sufferings until death. The paths that he travels with us and through which he leads us to life are pathways of hope.

When, in adoration, we look at the consecrated Host, the sign of creation speaks to us. And so, we encounter the greatness of his gift; but we also encounter the Passion, the Cross of Jesus and his Resurrection. Through this gaze of adoration, he draws us toward himself, within his mystery, through which he wants to transform us as he transformed the Host.

The primitive Church discovered yet another symbol in the bread. *The Doctrine of the Twelve Apostles,** a book written around the year 100, contains in its prayers the affirmation: "Even as this broken bread was scattered over the hills, and was gathered together and became one, so let Thy Church be gathered together from the ends of the earth into Thy Kingdom" (IX, 4).

Bread made of many grains contains also an event of union: the ground grain becoming bread is a process of unification. We ourselves, many as we are, must become one bread, one body, as St Paul says (cf. I Cor 10: 17). In this way the sign of bread becomes both hope and fulfilment. In a very similar way the sign of wine speaks to us. However, while bread speaks of daily life, simplicity and pilgrimage, wine expresses the exquisiteness of creation: the feast of joy that God wants to offer to us at the end of time and that already now and always anticipates anew a

----

* Commonly called the *Didache*.

foretaste through this sign.

But, wine also speaks of the Passion: the vine must be repeatedly pruned to be purified in this way; the grapes must mature with the sun and the rain and must be pressed: only through this passion does a fine wine mature.

On the feast of Corpus Christi we especially look at the sign of bread. It reminds us of the pilgrimage of Israel during the 40 years in the desert. The Host is our manna whereby the Lord nourishes us – it is truly the bread of heaven, through which he gives himself.

In the procession we follow this sign and in this way we follow Christ himself. And we ask of him: Guide us on the paths of our history! Show the Church and her Pastors again and again the right path! Look at suffering humanity, cautiously seeking a way through so much doubt; look upon the physical and mental hunger that torments it! Give men and women bread for body and soul! Give them work! Give them light! Give them yourself! Purify and sanctify all of us! Make us understand that only through participation in your Passion, through "yes" to the cross, to self-denial, to the purifications that you impose upon us, can our lives mature and arrive at true fulfilment. Gather us together from all corners of the earth. Unite your Church, unite wounded humanity! Give us your salvation! Amen.

MASS OF THE LORD'S SUPPER

Basilica of St John Lateran
Holy Thursday, 5 April 2007

The Passover

In the Reading from the Book of Exodus which we have just heard, the celebration of the Passover of Israel is described, just as in Mosaic Law it found its definitive form.

At the outset, it might have been a spring feast for nomads. For Israel, however, it was transformed into a commemorative feast of thanksgiving and, at the same time, hope.

The centre of the Passover meal, regulated by specific liturgical provisions, was the lamb as the symbol of Israel's redemption from slavery in Egypt.

For this reason the paschal *haggada* was an integral part of the Passover meal based on lamb: the narrative commemoration of the fact that it had been God himself who set Israel free by "stretching out his hand".

He, the mysterious and hidden God, had shown himself to be stronger than Pharaoh, in spite of all the power that Pharaoh could muster.

Israel was never to forget that God had personally taken the history of his People in hand and that this history was based permanently on communion with God. Israel must not forget God.

The words of the commemoration were surrounded by words of praise and thanksgiving taken from the Psalms. Thanking and blessing God reached its culmination in the *berakah,* which in

Greek is *eulogia* or *eucharistia:* praising God becomes a blessing for those who bless him. The offering given to God comes back blessed to man.

All this built a bridge from the past to the present and toward the future: Israel had not yet been liberated. The nation was still suffering, like a small people, in the sphere of tension between the great powers.

Thus, remembering with gratitude God's past action became at the same time supplication and hope: Bring to completion what you have begun! Grant us freedom once and for all!

It was on the eve of his Passion that Jesus together with his disciples celebrated this meal with its multiple meanings. This is the context in which we must understand the new Passover which he has given to us in the Blessed Eucharist.

There is an apparent discrepancy in the Evangelists' accounts, between John's Gospel on the one hand, and what on the other Matthew, Mark and Luke tell us.

According to John, Jesus died on the Cross at the very moment when the Passover lambs were being sacrificed in the temple. The death of Jesus and the sacrifice of the lambs coincided. However, this means that he must have died the day before Easter and could not, therefore, have celebrated the Passover meal in person – this, at any rate, is how it appears.

According to the three Synoptic Gospels, the Last Supper of Jesus was instead a Passover meal into whose traditional form he integrated the innovation of the gift of his Body and Blood.

This contradiction seemed unsolvable until a few years ago. The majority of exegetes were of the opinion that John was reluctant to tell us the true historical date of Jesus' death, but rather chose a symbolic date to highlight the deeper truth: Jesus is the new, true Lamb who poured out his Blood for us all.

In the meantime, the discovery of the [Dead Sea] Scrolls at Qumran has led us to a possible and convincing solution which, although it is not yet accepted by everyone, is a highly plausible hypothesis. We can now say that John's account is historically precise.

Jesus truly shed his blood on the eve of Easter at the time of the immolation of the lambs. In all likelihood, however, he celebrated the Passover with his disciples in accordance with the Qumran calendar, hence, at least one day earlier; he celebrated it without a lamb, like the Qumran community which did not recognize Herod's temple and was waiting for the new temple.

Consequently, Jesus celebrated the Passover without a lamb – no, not without a lamb: instead of the lamb he gave himself, his Body and his Blood. Thus, he anticipated his death in a manner consistent with his words: "No one takes [my life] from me, but I lay it down of my own accord" (Jn 10: 18).

At the time when he offered his Body and his Blood to the disciples, he was truly fulfilling this affirmation. He himself offered his own life. Only in this way did the ancient Passover acquire its true meaning.

In his Eucharistic catecheses, St John Chrysostom once wrote: "Moses, what are you saying? Does the blood of a lamb purify men and women? Does it save them from death? How can the blood of an animal purify people, save people or have power over death?" In fact, Chrysostom continues, the immolation of the lamb could be a merely symbolic act, hence, the expression of expectation and hope in One who could accomplish what the sacrifice of an animal was incapable of accomplishing.

The Lamb and Temple

Jesus celebrated the Passover without a lamb and without a temple; yet, not without a lamb and not without a temple. He himself was the awaited Lamb, the true Lamb, just as John the Baptist had foretold at the beginning of Jesus' public ministry: "Behold, the Lamb of God, who takes away the sin of the world!" (Jn 1: 29).

And he himself was the true Temple, the living Temple where God dwells and where we can encounter God and worship him. His Blood, the love of the One who is both Son of God and true man, one of us, is the Blood that can save. His love, that love in which he gave himself freely for us, is what saves us. The nostalgic, in a certain sense, ineffectual gesture which was the sacrifice of an innocent and perfect lamb, found a response in the One who for our sake became at the same time Lamb and Temple.

Thus, the Cross was at the centre of the new Passover of Jesus. From it came the new gift brought by him, and so it lives on for ever in the Blessed Eucharist in which, down the ages, we can celebrate the new Passover with the Apostles.

From Christ's Cross comes the gift. "No one takes [my life] from me, but I lay it down of my own accord." He now offers it to us.

The paschal *haggada,* the commemoration of God's saving action, has become a memorial of the Cross and Resurrection of Christ – a memorial that does not simply recall the past but attracts us within the presence of Christ's love.

Thus, the *berakah,* Israel's prayer of blessing and thanksgiving, has become our Eucharistic Celebration in which the Lord blesses our gifts – the bread and wine – to give himself in them. Let us pray to the Lord that he will help us to understand this marvellous mystery ever more profoundly, to love it more and more, and in it, to love the Lord himself ever more.

Let us pray that he will increasingly draw us to himself with Holy Communion. Let us pray that he will help us not to keep our life for ourselves but to give it to him and thus to work with him so that people may find life: the true life which can only come from the One who himself is the Way, the Truth and the Life. Amen.

Homily given during the

HOLY MASS AND EUCHARISTIC PROCESSION TO THE BASILICA OF SAINT MARY MAJOR ON THE SOLEMNITY OF CORPUS CHRISTI

Square in front of the Basilica of Saint John Lateran
Thursday, 7 June 2007

The Bread of Angels

We have just sung the Sequence: *"Dogma datur christianis, / quod in carnem transit panis, / et vinum in sanguinem* – this [is] the truth each Christian learns, / bread into his flesh he turns, / to his precious blood the wine".

Today we reaffirm with great joy our faith in the Eucharist, the Mystery that constitutes the heart of the Church. In the recent Post-Synodal Apostolic Exhortation *Sacramentum Caritatis* I recalled that the Eucharistic Mystery "is the gift that Jesus Christ makes of himself, thus revealing to us God's infinite love for every man and woman" (n. 1).

Corpus Christi, therefore, is a unique feast and constitutes an important encounter of faith and praise for every Christian community. This feast originated in a specific historical and cultural context: it was born for the very precise purpose of openly reaffirming the faith of the People of God in Jesus Christ, alive and truly present in the Most Holy Sacrament of the Eucharist. It is a feast that was established in order to publicly adore, praise and thank the Lord, who continues "to love us 'to the end', even to offering us his body and his blood" (*Sacramentum Caritatis*, n. 1).

The Eucharistic celebration this evening takes us back to the spiritual atmosphere of Holy Thursday, the day on which in the Upper Room, on the eve of his Passion, Christ instituted the Most Holy Eucharist.

Corpus Christi is thus a renewal of the mystery of Holy Thursday, as it were, in obedience to Jesus' invitation to proclaim from "the housetops" what he told us in secret (cf. Mt 10: 27). It was the Apostles who received the gift of the Eucharist from the Lord in the intimacy of the Last Supper, but it was destined for all, for the whole world. This is why it should be proclaimed and exposed to view: so that each one may encounter "Jesus who passes" as happened on the roads of Galilee, Samaria and Judea; in order that each one, in receiving it, may be healed and renewed by the power of his love. Dear friends, this is the perpetual and living heritage that Jesus has bequeathed to us in the Sacrament of his Body and his Blood. It is an inheritance that demands to be constantly rethought and relived so that, as venerable Pope Paul VI said, its "inexhaustible effectiveness may be impressed upon all the days of our mortal life" (cf. *Insegnamenti,* 25 May 1967, p. 779).

Also in the Post-Synodal Exhortation, commenting on the exclamation of the priest after the consecration: "Let us proclaim the mystery of faith!" I observed: with these words he "proclaims the mystery being celebrated and expresses his wonder before the substantial change of bread and wine into the body and blood of the Lord Jesus, a reality which surpasses all human understanding" (n. 6).

Precisely because this is a mysterious reality that surpasses our understanding, we must not be surprised if today too many find it hard to accept the Real Presence of Christ in the Eucharist. It cannot be otherwise. This is how it has been since the day when, in the synagogue at Capernaum, Jesus openly declared that he had come to give us his flesh and his blood as food (cf. Jn 6: 26-58). This seemed "a hard saying" and many of his disciples withdrew when they heard it. Then, as now, the Eucharist remains a "sign of contradiction" and can only be so because a God who makes himself flesh and sacrifices himself for the life of the world throws human wisdom into crisis.

However, with humble trust, the Church makes the faith of Peter and the other Apostles her own and proclaims with them, and we proclaim: "Lord, to whom shall we go? You have the words of eternal life" (Jn 6: 68). Let us too renew this evening our profession of faith in Christ, alive and present in the Eucharist. Yes, "this [is] the truth each Christian learns, / bread into his flesh he turns, / to his precious blood the wine".

At its culminating point, in the Sequence we sing: *"Ecce panis angelorum, / factus cibus viatorum: / vere panis filiorum"* – "Lo! The angel's food is given / to the pilgrim who has striven; / see the children's bread from heaven". And by God's grace we are the children.

The Eucharist is the food reserved for those who in Baptism were delivered from slavery and have become sons; it is the food that sustained them on the long journey of the exodus through the desert of human existence.

Like the manna for the people of Israel, for every Christian generation the Eucharist is the indispensable nourishment that sustains them as they cross the desert of this world, parched by the ideological and economic systems that do not promote life but rather humiliate it. It is a world where the logic of power and possessions prevails rather than that of service and love; a world where the culture of violence and death is frequently triumphant.

Yet Jesus comes to meet us and imbues us with certainty: he himself is "the Bread of life" (Jn 6: 35, 48). He repeated this to us in the words of the Gospel Acclamation: "I am the living bread from Heaven, if any one eats of this bread, he will live for ever" (cf. Jn 6: 51).

In the Gospel passage just proclaimed, St Luke, narrating the miracle of the multiplication of the five loaves and two fish with which Jesus fed the multitude "in a lonely place", concludes with the words: "And all ate and were satisfied" (cf. Lk 9: 11-17).

I would like in the first place to emphasize this "all". Indeed, the Lord desired every human being to be nourished by the Eucharist, because the Eucharist is for everyone.

If the close relationship between the Last Supper and the mystery of Jesus' death on the Cross is emphasized on Holy Thursday, today, the Feast of Corpus Christi, with the procession and unanimous adoration of the Eucharist, attention is called to the fact that Christ sacrificed himself for all humanity. His passing among the houses and along the streets of our city will be for those who live there an offering of joy, eternal life, peace and love.

In the Gospel passage, a second element catches one's eye: the miracle worked by the Lord contains an explicit invitation to each person to make his own contribution. The two fish and five loaves signify our contribution, poor but necessary, which he transforms into a gift of love for all. "Christ continues today" I wrote in the above-mentioned Post Synodal Exhortation, "to exhort his disciples to become personally engaged" (*Sacramentum Caritatis,* n. 88).

Thus, the Eucharist is a call to holiness and to the gift of oneself to one's brethren: "Each of us is truly called, together with Jesus, to be bread broken for the life of the world" (ibid.).

Our Redeemer addressed this invitation in particular to us, dear brothers and sisters of Rome, gathered round the Eucharist in this historic square.

At the end of the Eucharistic celebration we will join in the procession as if to carry the Lord Jesus in spirit through all the streets and neighbourhoods of Rome. We will immerse him, so to speak, in the daily routine of our lives, so that he may walk where we walk and live where we live.

Indeed we know, as the Apostle Paul reminded us in his Letter to the Corinthians, that in every Eucharist, also in the Eucharist this evening, we "proclaim the Lord's death until he comes" (cf. I Cor 11: 26). We travel on the highways of the world knowing that he is beside us, supported by the hope of being able to see him one day face to face, in the definitive encounter.

In the meantime, let us listen to his voice repeat, as we read in the Book of Revelation, "Behold, I stand at the door and knock; if any one hears my voice and opens the door, I will come in to him and eat with him, and he with me" (Rev 3: 20).

The Feast of Corpus Christi wants to make the Lord's knocking audible, despite the hardness of our interior hearing. Jesus knocks at the door of our heart and asks to enter not only for the space of a day but for ever. Let us welcome him joyfully, raising to him with one voice the invocation of the Liturgy:

"Very bread, Good Shepherd, tend us, / Jesu, of your love befriend us. . . . / You who all things can and know, /who on earth such food bestow, / grant us with your saints, though lowest, / where the heav'nly feast you show, / fellow heirs and guests to be".

Amen!

HOLY MASS AND EUCHARISTIC PROCESSION TO THE BASILICA OF SAINT MARY MAJOR ON THE SOLEMNITY OF CORPUS CHRISTI

Square in front of the Basilica of Saint John Lateran
Thursday, 22 May 2008

In His Presence

After the strong season of the liturgical year which, focusing on Easter spreads over three months – first the 40 days of Lent, then the 50 days of Eastertide – the liturgy has us celebrate three Feasts which instead have a "synthetic" character: the Most Holy Trinity, then Corpus Christi, and lastly, the Sacred Heart of Jesus. What is the precise significance of today's Solemnity, of the Body and Blood of Christ? The answer is given to us in the fundamental actions of this celebration we are carrying out: first of all we *gather* around the altar of the Lord, to *be together in his presence;* secondly, there will be the procession, that is *walking with the Lord;* and lastly, *kneeling before the Lord,* adoration, which already begins in the Mass and accompanies the entire procession but culminates in the final moment of the Eucharistic Blessing when we all prostrate ourselves before the One who stooped down to us and gave his life for us. Let us reflect briefly on these three attitudes, so that they may truly be an expression of our faith and our life.

The first action, therefore, is *to gather together* in the Lord's presence. This is what in former times was called *"statio"*. Let us imagine for a moment that in the whole of Rome there were only this one altar and that all the city's Christians were invited to gather here to celebrate the Saviour who died and was raised. This gives us an idea of what the Eucharistic celebration must have been like at the origins, in Rome and in many other cities that the Gospel message had reached. In every particular Church there was only one bishop and around him, around the Eucharist that he celebrated, a community was formed, one, because one was the blessed Cup and one was the Bread broken, as we heard in the Apostle Paul's words in the Second Reading (cf. I Cor 10: 16-17). That other famous Pauline expression comes to mind: "There is neither Jew nor Greek, there is neither slave nor free, there is neither male nor female; for you are all one in Christ Jesus" (Gal 3: 28). "You are all one!" In these words the truth and power of the Christian revolution is heard, the most profound revolution of human history, which was experienced precisely around the Eucharist: here people of different age groups, sex, social background, and political ideas gather together in the Lord's presence. The Eucharist can never be a private event, reserved for people chosen through affinity or friendship. The Eucharist is a public devotion that has nothing esoteric or exclusive about it. Here too, this evening, we did not choose to meet one another, we came and find ourselves next to one another, brought together by faith and called to become one body, sharing the one Bread which is Christ. We are united over and above our differences of nationality, profession, social class, political ideas: we open ourselves to one another to become one in him. This has been a characteristic of Christianity from the outset, visibly fulfilled around the Eucharist, and it is always necessary to be alert to ensure that the recurring temptations of particularism, even if with good intentions, do not go in the opposite direction. Therefore Corpus Christi reminds us first of all of this: that being Christian means coming together from all parts of the world to be in the presence of the one Lord and to become one with him and in him.

The second constitutive aspect is *walking with the Lord*. This is the reality manifested by the procession that we shall experience together after Holy Mass, almost as if it were naturally prolonged by moving behind the One who is the Way, the Journey. With the gift of himself in the Eucharist the Lord Jesus sets us free from our "paralyses", he helps us up and enables us to "proceed", that is, he makes us take a step ahead and then another step, and thus sets us going with the power of the Bread of Life. As happened to the Prophet Elijah who had sought refuge in the wilderness for fear of his enemies and had made up his mind to let himself die (cf. I Kgs 19: 1-4). But God awoke him from sleep and caused him to find beside him a freshly baked loaf: "Arise and eat", the angel said, "else the journey will be too great for you" (I Kgs 19: 5,7). The Corpus Christi procession teaches us that the Eucharist seeks to free us from every kind of despondency and discouragement, wants to raise us, so that we can set out on the journey with the strength God gives us through Jesus Christ. It is the experience of the People of Israel in the exodus from Egypt, their long wandering through the desert, as the First Reading relates. It is an experience which was constitutive for Israel but is exemplary for all humanity. Indeed the saying: "Man does not live by bread alone, but . . . by everything that proceeds out of the mouth of the Lord" (Dt 8: 3), is a universal affirmation which refers to every man or woman as a person. Each one can find his own way if he encounters the One who is the Word and the Bread of Life and lets himself be guided by his friendly presence. Without the God-with-us, the God who is close, how can we stand up to the pilgrimage through life, either on our own or as society and the family of peoples? The Eucharist is the Sacrament of the God who does not leave us alone on the journey but stays at our side and shows us the way. Indeed, it is not enough to move onwards, one must also see where one is going! "Progress" does not suffice, if there are no criteria as reference points. On the contrary, if one loses the way one risks coming to a precipice, or at any rate more rapidly distancing oneself from the goal. God created us free but he did not leave us alone: he made himself the "way" and came to walk together with us so that in our freedom we should also have the criterion we need to discern the right way and to take it.

At this point we cannot forget the beginning of the Decalogue, the Ten Commandments, where it is written: "I am the Lord your God, who brought you out of the land of Egypt, out of the house of bondage. You shall have no other gods before me" (Ex 20: 2-3). Here we find the meaning of the third constitutive element of Corpus Christi: kneeling in adoration before the Lord. Adoring the God of Jesus Christ, who out of love made himself bread broken, is the most effective and radical remedy against the idolatry of the past and of the present. Kneeling before the Eucharist is a profession of freedom: those who bow to Jesus cannot and must not prostrate themselves before any earthly authority, however powerful. We Christians kneel only before God or before the Most Blessed Sacrament because we know and believe that the one true God is present in it, the God who created the world and so loved it that he gave his Only Begotten Son (cf. Jn 3: 16). We prostrate ourselves before a God who first bent over man like the Good Samaritan to assist him and restore his life, and who knelt before us to wash our dirty feet. Adoring the Body of Christ, means believing that there, in that piece of Bread, Christ is really there, and gives true sense to life, to the immense universe as to the smallest creature, to the whole of human history as to the most brief existence. Adoration is prayer that prolongs the celebration and Eucharistic communion and in which the soul continues to be nourished: it is nourished with love, truth, peace; it is nourished with hope, because the One before whom we prostrate ourselves does not judge us, does not crush us but liberates and transforms us.

This is why gathering, walking and adoring together fills us with joy. In making our own the adoring attitude of Mary, whom we especially remember in this month of May, let us pray for ourselves and for everyone; let us pray for every person who lives in this city, that he or she may know you, O Father and the One whom you sent, Jesus Christ and thus have life in abundance. Amen.

From the Homily given during a

LIVE BROADCAST VIA SATELLITE FOR THE CLOSING OF THE 49th INTERNATIONAL EUCHARISTIC CONFERENCE IN QUÉBEC (CANADA)

Foconi Hall
Sunday, 22 June 2008

'The Eucharist, gift of God for the life of the World'

"The Eucharist, gift of God for the life of the world" is the theme chosen for this new International Eucharistic Congress. The Eucharist is our most beautiful treasure. It is the Sacrament *par excellence*; it ushers us into eternal life in advance; it contains the entire mystery of our salvation; it is the source and summit of the action and life of the Church as the Second Vatican Council recalled (cf. *Sacrosanctum Concilium*, n. 8). It is therefore particularly important that pastors and faithful be constantly committed to deepening their knowledge of this great Sacrament. In this way each one will be able to affirm his faith and carry out his mission in the Church and in the world ever better, remembering that the Eucharist bears fruit in one's personal life, in the life of the Church and the world. The Spirit of truth bears witness in your hearts; may you too witness to Christ among men and women, as the Gospel acclamation of this Mass says. Thus, participation in the Eucharist does not distance our contemporaries. On the contrary, since it is the expression par excellence of God's love, it calls us to join forces with all our brothers and sisters to confront today's challenges and make the earth a place that is pleasant to live in. This requires that we constantly fight to ensure that everyone is respected, from conception until natural death, that our rich societies welcome the poorest and restore dignity to all, that everyone has food and can enable his family to survive and that peace and justice shine out on all the continents. These are some of the challenges that must mobilize all our contemporaries, and from the Eucharistic mystery Christians must draw the strength to confront them.

The "Mystery of Faith": this we proclaim at every Mass. I would like everyone to make a commitment to study this great mystery, especially by revisiting and exploring, individually and in groups, the Council's text on the Liturgy, *Sacrosanctum Concilium*, so as to bear witness courageously to the mystery. In this way, each person will arrive at a better grasp of the meaning of every aspect of the Eucharist, understanding its depth and living it with greater intensity. Every sentence, every gesture has its own meaning and conceals a mystery. I sincerely hope that this Congress will serve as an appeal to all the faithful to make a similar commitment to a renewal of Eucharistic catechesis, so that they themselves will gain a genuine Eucharistic awareness and will in turn teach children and young people to recognize the central mystery of faith and build their lives around it. I urge priests especially to give due honour to the Eucharistic rite, and I ask all the faithful to respect the role of each individual, both priest and lay, in the Eucharistic action. The liturgy does not belong to us: it is the Church's treasure.

Reception of the Eucharist, adoration of the Blessed Sacrament – by this we mean deepening our Communion, preparing for it and prolonging it – is also about allowing ourselves to enter into communion with Christ, and through him with the whole of the Trinity, so as to become what we receive and to live in communion with the Church. It is by receiving the Body of Christ that we receive the strength "of unity with God and with one another" (St Cyril of Alexandria, *In Ioannis Evangelium*, 11: 11; cf. St Augustine, *Sermo* 577). We must never forget that the Church is built around Christ and that, as St Augustine, St Thomas Aquinas and St Albert the Great have all said, following St Paul (cf. 1 Cor 10: 17), the Eucharist is the Sacrament of the Church's unity, because we all form one single body of which the Lord is the head. We must go back again and again to the Last Supper on Holy Thursday, where we were given a pledge of the mystery of our redemption on the Cross. The Last Supper is the locus of the nascent Church, the womb containing the Church of every age. In the Eucharist, Christ's sacrifice is constantly renewed, Pentecost is constantly renewed. May all of you become ever more deeply aware of the importance of the Sunday Eucharist, because Sunday, the first day of the week, is the day when we honour Christ, the day when we receive the strength to live each day the gift of God.

I would also like to invite pastors and the faithful to take a renewed interest in their preparation for receiving the Eucharist. Despite our weakness and sin, Christ wants to make his dwelling place in us. This is why we must do everything in our power to receive him with a pure heart, continuously rediscovering through the Sacrament of forgiveness that purity which sin has stained, "that [our] minds be attuned to [our] voices" (cf. *Sacrosanctum Concilium,* n. 11), according to the Council's invitation. Sin in fact, especially serious sin, impedes the action of Eucharistic grace within us. Moreover, those who cannot receive Communion because of their situation will find a saving power and effectiveness in a Communion of desire and from participation at the Eucharist.

The Eucharist has a very special place in the life of Saints. Let us thank God for the history of holiness of Quebec and of Canada, which has contributed to the missionary life of the Church. Your Country honours in particular its Canadian martyrs, John Brébeuf, Isaac Jogues and their companions who were able to give their lives for Christ, thereby associating themselves with his sacrifice on the Cross. They belong to the generation of men and women who founded and developed the Church in Canada, with Marguerite Bourgeoys, Marguerite d'Youville, Marie of the Incarnation, Marie Catherine of St Augustine, Bishop François de Laval, founder of the first diocese in North America, Dina Bélanger and Kateri Tekakwitha. Learn from them and, like them, be fearless; God accompanies and protects you; every day make an offering for the glory of God the Father and play your part in the construction of the world, proudly remembering your religious heritage and its social and cultural outreach, and taking care to spread around you the moral and spiritual values that come to us from the Lord.

The Eucharist is not a meal with friends. It is the mystery of a covenant. "The prayers and rites of the Eucharistic sacrifice revive the whole history of salvation continuously before the eyes of our soul, in the course of the liturgical cycle and make us enter its significance ever more deeply" (St Teresa Benedicta of the Cross [Edith Stein], *Wege zu inneren Stille,* Aschaffenburg, 1987, p. 67). We are called to enter into this mystery of a covenant by conforming our lives ever more closely each day to the gift received in the Eucharist. It has a sacred character, as the Second Vatican Council recalls: "every liturgical celebration, because it is an action of Christ the Priest and of his Body, which is the Church, is a sacred action surpassing all others. No other action of the Church can equal its efficacy by the same title and to the same degree" (*Sacrosanctum Concilium,* n. 7). In a certain way, it is a "heavenly liturgy", an anticipation of the banquet in the eternal Kingdom, announcing the death and Resurrection of

Christ "until he comes" (1 Cor 11: 26).

In order that the People of God may never lack ministers to give them the Body of Christ, we must ask the Lord to make the gift of new priests to his Church. I also ask you to pass on the call to the priesthood to young men, so that they will joyfully and fearlessly respond to the Lord. They will not be disappointed. May the family be the origin and cradle of vocations. I ask the Lord to enable each one of you to discover the depth and grandeur of the mystery of faith. May Christ, present in the Eucharist, and the Holy Spirit invoked upon the bread and the wine, accompany you on your daily journey and in your mission. May you be ready for God to work within you, after the example of the Virgin Mary.

APOSTOLIC JOURNEY OF HIS HOLINESS
BENEDICT XVI TO FRANCE ON THE
OCCASION OF THE 150th ANNIVERSARY
OF THE APPARITIONS OF THE BLESSED
VIRGIN MARY AT LOURDES
(12-15 SEPTEMBER 2008)

From the Homily given during

HOLY MASS

*Notre-Dame, Esplanade des Invalides, Paris
Saturday, 13 September 2008*

'I will raise the cup of salvation'

How do we reach God? How do we manage to discover or rediscover him whom man seeks at the deepest core of himself, even though he so often forgets him? Saint Paul asks us to make use not only of our reason, but above all our faith in order to discover him. Now, what does faith say to us? The bread that we break is a communion with the Body of Christ. The cup of blessing which we bless is a communion with the Blood of Christ. This extraordinary revelation comes to us from Christ and has been transmitted to us by the Apostles and by the whole Church for almost two thousand years: Christ instituted the Sacrament of the Eucharist on the evening of Holy Thursday. He wanted his sacrifice to be presented anew, in an unbloody manner, every time a priest repeats the words of consecration over the bread and wine. Millions of times over the last twenty centuries, in the humblest chapels and in the most magnificent basilicas and cathedrals, the risen Lord has given himself to his people, thus becoming, in the famous expression of Saint Augustine, "more intimate to us than we are to ourselves" (cf. *Confessions,* III, 6, 11).

Brothers and sisters, let us give the greatest veneration to the Sacrament of the Body and Blood of the Lord, the Blessed Sacrament of the Real Presence of the Lord to his Church and to all humanity. Let us take every opportunity to show him our respect and our love! Let us give him the greatest marks of honour! Through our words, our silences, and our gestures, let us never allow our faith in the risen Christ, present in the Eucharist, to lose its savour in us or around us! As Saint John Chrysostom said magnificently, "Let us behold the ineffable generosity of God and all the good things that he enables us to enjoy, when we offer him this cup, when we receive Communion, thanking him for having delivered the human race from error, for having brought close to him those who were far away, for having made, out of those who were without hope and without God in the world, a people of brothers, fellow heirs with the Son of God" (Homily 24 on the First Letter to the Corinthians, 1). "In fact", he continues, "what is in the cup is precisely what flowed from his side, and it is of this that we partake" (ibid.). There is not only partaking and sharing, there is "union", says the Doctor whose name means "golden mouth".

The Mass is the sacrifice of thanksgiving par excellence, the one which allows us to unite our own thanksgiving to that of the Saviour, the Eternal Son of the Father. It also makes its own appeal to us to shun idols, for, as Saint Paul insists, "you cannot partake of the table of the Lord and the table of demons" (I Cor 10: 21). The Mass invites us to discern what, in ourselves, is obedient to the Spirit of God and what, in ourselves, is attuned to the spirit of evil. In the Mass, we want to belong only to

Christ and we take up with gratitude – with thanksgiving – the cry of the psalmist: "How shall I repay the Lord for his goodness to me?" (Ps 116: 12). Yes, how can I give thanks to the Lord for the life he has given me? The answer to the psalmist's question is found in the psalm itself, since the word of God responds graciously to its own questions. How else could we render thanks to the Lord for all his goodness to us if not by attending to his own words: "I will raise the cup of salvation, I will call on the name of the Lord" (Ps 116: 13)?

To raise the cup of salvation and call on the name of the Lord, is that not the very best way of "shunning idols", as Saint Paul asks us to do? Every time the Mass is celebrated, every time Christ makes himself sacramentally present in his Church, the work of our salvation is accomplished. Hence to celebrate the Eucharist means to recognize that God alone has the power to grant us the fullness of joy and teach us true values, eternal values that will never pass away. God is present on the altar, but he is also present on the altar of our heart when, as we receive Communion, we receive him in the Sacrament of the Eucharist. He alone teaches us to shun idols, the illusions of our minds.

MASS OF THE LORD'S SUPPER

Basilica of St John Lateran
Holy Thursday, 9 April 2009

The Canon of the Mass

Qui, pridie quam pro nostra omniumque salute pateretur, hoc est hodie, accepit panem: these words we shall pray today in the Canon of the Mass. "*Hoc est hodie*" – the Liturgy of Holy Thursday places the word "today" into the text of the prayer, thereby emphasizing the particular dignity of this day. It was "today" that He did this: he gave himself to us for ever in the Sacrament of his Body and Blood. This "today" is first and foremost the memorial of that first Paschal event. Yet it is something more. With the Canon, we enter into this "today". Our today comes into contact with his today. He does this now. With the word "today", the Church's Liturgy wants us to give great inner attention to the mystery of this day, to the words in which it is expressed. We therefore seek to listen in a new way to the institution narrative, in the form in which the Church has formulated it, on the basis of Scripture and in contemplation of the Lord himself.

The first thing to strike us is that the institution narrative is not an independent phrase, but it starts with a relative pronoun: *qui pridie*. This "*qui*" connects the entire narrative to the preceding section of the prayer, "let it become for us the body and blood of Jesus Christ, your only Son, our Lord." In this way, the institution narrative is linked to the preceding prayer, to the entire Canon, and it too becomes a prayer. By no means is it merely an interpolated narrative, nor is it a case of an authoritative self-standing text that actually interrupts the prayer. It *is* a prayer. And only in the course of the prayer is the priestly act of consecration accomplished, which becomes transformation, transubstantiation of our gifts of bread and wine into the Body and Blood of Christ. As she prays at this central moment, the Church is fully in tune with the event that took place in the Upper Room, when Jesus' action is described in the words: "*gratias agens benedixit* – he gave you thanks and praise". In this expression, the Roman liturgy has made two words out of the one Hebrew word *berakah*, which is rendered in Greek with the two terms *eucharistía* and *eulogía*. The Lord gives thanks. When we thank, we acknowledge that a certain thing is a gift that has come from another. The Lord gives thanks, and in so doing gives back to God the bread, "fruit of the earth and work of human hands", so as to receive it anew from him. Thanksgiving becomes blessing. The offering that we have placed in God's hands returns from him blessed and transformed. The Roman liturgy rightly interprets, therefore, our praying at this sacred moment by means of the words: "through him, we ask you to accept and bless these gifts we offer you in sacrifice". All this lies hidden within the word "*eucharistia*".

There is another aspect of the institution narrative cited in the Roman Canon on which we should reflect this evening. The praying Church gazes upon the hands and eyes of the Lord. It is as if she wants to observe him, to perceive the form of his praying and acting in that remarkable hour, she wants to encounter the figure of Jesus even, as it were, through the senses. "He took bread in his sacred hands . . ." Let us look at those hands with which he healed men and women; the hands with which he blessed babies; the hands that he laid upon men; the hands that were nailed to the Cross and that forever bear the stigmata as signs of his readiness to die for love. Now we are commissioned to do what he did: to take bread in our hands so that through the Eucharistic Prayer it will be transformed.

At our priestly ordination, our hands were anointed, so that they could become hands of blessing. Let us pray to the Lord at this hour that our hands will serve more and more to bring salvation, to bring blessing, to make his goodness present!

From the introduction to the Priestly Prayer of Jesus (cf. Jn 17: 1), the Canon takes these words: "Looking up to heaven, to you his almighty Father . . ." The Lord teaches us to raise our eyes, and especially our hearts. He teaches us to fix our gaze upwards, detaching it from the things of this world, to direct ourselves in prayer towards God and thus to raise ourselves. In a hymn from the Liturgy of the Hours, we ask the Lord to guard our eyes, so that they do not take in or cause to enter within us "*vanitates*" – vanities, nothings, that which is merely appearance. Let us pray that no evil will enter through our eyes, falsifying and tainting our very being. But we want to pray above all for eyes that see whatever is true, radiant and good; so that they become capable of seeing God's presence in the world. Let us pray that we will look upon the world with eyes of love, with the eyes of Jesus, recognizing our brothers and sisters who need our help, who are awaiting our word and our action.

Having given thanks and praise, the Lord then breaks the bread and gives it to the disciples. Breaking the bread is the act of the father of the family who looks after his children and gives them what they need for life. But it is also the act of hospitality with which the stranger, the guest, is received within the family and is given a share in its life. Dividing (*dividere*), sharing (*condividere*) brings about unity. Through sharing, communion is created. In the broken bread, the Lord distributes himself. The gesture of breaking also alludes mysteriously to his death, to the love that extends even to death. He distributes himself, the true "bread for the life of the world" (cf. Jn 6: 51). The nourishment that man needs in his deepest self is communion with God himself. Giving thanks and praise, Jesus transforms the bread, he no longer gives earthly bread, but communion with himself. This transformation, though, seeks to be the start of the transformation of the world – into a world of resurrection, a world of God. Yes, it is about transformation – of the new man and the new world that find their origin in the bread that is consecrated, transformed, transubstantiated.

We said that breaking the bread is an act of communion, an act of uniting through sharing. Thus, in the act itself, the intimate nature of the Eucharist is already indicated: it is *agape*, it is love made corporeal. In the word *"agape"*, the meanings of Eucharist and love intertwine. In Jesus' act of breaking the bread, the love that is shared has attained its most radical form: Jesus allows himself to be broken as living bread. In the bread that is distributed, we recognize the mystery of the grain of wheat that dies, and so bears fruit. We recognize the new multiplication of the loaves, which derives from the dying of the grain of wheat and will continue until the end of the world. At the same time, we see that the Eucharist can never be just a liturgical action. It is complete only if the liturgical *agape* then becomes love in daily life. In Christian worship, the two things become one – experiencing the Lord's love in the act of worship and fostering love for one's neighbour. At this hour, we ask the Lord for the grace to learn to live the mystery of the Eucharist ever more deeply, in such a way that the transformation of the world can begin to take place.

After the bread, Jesus takes the chalice of wine. The Roman Canon describes the chalice which the Lord gives to his disciples as *"praeclarus calix"* (the glorious cup), thereby alluding to Psalm 23 [22], the Psalm which speaks of God as the Good Shepherd, the strong Shepherd. There we read these words: "You have prepared a banquet for me in the sight of my foes. . . . My cup is overflowing" – *calix praeclarus*. The Roman Canon interprets this passage from the Psalm as a prophecy that is fulfilled in the Eucharist: yes, the Lord does indeed prepare a banquet for us in the midst of the threats of this world, and he gives us the glorious chalice – the chalice of great joy, of the true feast, for which we all long – the chalice filled with the wine of his love. The chalice signifies the wedding-feast: now the "hour" has come to which the wedding-feast of Cana had mysteriously alluded. Yes indeed, the Eucharist is more than a meal, it is a wedding-feast. And this wedding is rooted in God's gift of himself even to death. In the words of Jesus at the Last Supper and in the Church's Canon, the solemn mystery of the wedding is concealed under the expression "*novum Testamentum*". This chalice is the new Testament – "the new Covenant in my blood", as Saint Paul presents the words of Jesus over the chalice in today's second reading (I Cor 11: 25). The Roman Canon adds: "of the new and everlasting covenant", in order to express the indissolubility of God's nuptial bond with humanity. The reason why older translations of the Bible do not say Covenant, but Testament, lies in the fact that this is no mere contract between two parties on the same level, but it brings into play the infinite distance between God and man. What we call the new and the ancient Covenant is not an agreement between two equal parties, but simply the gift of God who bequeaths to us his love – himself. Certainly, through this gift of his love, he transcends all distance and makes us truly his "partners" – the nuptial mystery of love is accomplished.

In order to understand profoundly what is taking place here, we must pay even greater attention to the words of the Bible and their original meaning. Scholars tell us that in those ancient times of which the histories of Israel's forefathers speak, to "ratify a Covenant" means "to enter with others into a bond based on blood or to welcome the other into one's own covenant fellowship and thus to enter into a communion of mutual rights and obligations." In this way, a real, if non-material form of consanguinity is established. The partners become in some way "brothers of the same flesh and the same bones". The covenant brings about a fellowship that means peace. Can we now form at least an idea of what happened at the hour of the Last Supper, and what has been renewed ever since, whenever we celebrate the Eucharist? God, the living God, establishes a communion of peace with us, or to put it more strongly, he creates "consanguinity" between himself and us. Through the Incarnation of Jesus, through the outpouring of his blood, we have been drawn into an utterly real consanguinity with Jesus and thus with God himself. The blood of Jesus is his love, in which divine life and human life have become one. Let us pray to the Lord, that we may come to understand ever more deeply the greatness of this mystery. Let us pray that in our innermost selves its transforming power will increase, so that we truly acquire consanguinity with Jesus, so that we are filled with his peace and grow in communion with one another.

Now, however, a further question arises. In the Upper Room, Christ gives his Body and Blood to the disciples, that is, he gives himself in the totality of his person. But can he do so? He is still physically present in their midst, he is standing in front of them! The answer is: at that hour, Jesus fulfils what he had previously proclaimed in the Good Shepherd discourse: "No one takes my life from me: I lay it down of my own accord. I have power to lay it down and I have power to take it again . . ." (Jn 10: 18). No one can take his life from him: he lays it down by his own free decision. At that hour, he anticipates the crucifixion and Resurrection. What is later to be fulfilled, as it were, physically in him, he already accomplishes in anticipation, in the freedom of his love. He gives his life and he takes it again in the Resurrection, so as to be able to share it for ever.

Lord, today you give us your life, you give us yourself. Enter deeply within us with your love. Make us live in your "today". Make us instruments of your peace!

Amen.

HOLY MASS FOR THE CANONIZATION OF FIVE NEW SAINTS

Arcangelo Tadini (1846-1912)
Bernardo Tolomei (1272-1348)
Nuno de Santa Maria Alvares Pereira (1360-1431)
Geltrude Comensoli (1847-1903)
Caterina Volpicelli (1839-1894)

St Peter's Square
Third Sunday of Easter, 26 April 2009

'Nourished with the Eucharistic Bread'

On this Third Sunday in the Easter Season, the liturgy once again focuses our attention on the mystery of the Risen Christ. Victorious over evil and over death, the Author of life who sacrificed himself as a victim of expiation for our sins, "is still our priest, our advocate who always pleads our cause. Christ is the victim who dies no more, the Lamb, once slain, who lives for ever" (Easter Preface III). Let us allow ourselves to be bathed in the radiance of Easter that shines from this great mystery and with the Responsorial Psalm let us pray: "O Lord, let the light of your countenance shine upon us".

The light of the face of the Risen Christ shines upon us today especially through the Gospel features of the five Blesseds who during this celebration are enrolled in the Roll of Saints: Arcangelo

Tadini, Bernardo Tolomei, Nuno de Santa Maria Alvares Pereira, Geltrude Comensoli and Caterina Volpicelli. The various human and spiritual experiences of these new Saints show us the profound renewal that the mystery of Christ's Resurrection brings about in the human heart; it is a fundamental mystery that orients and guides the entire history of salvation. The Church therefore, especially in this Easter Season, rightly invites us to direct our gaze to the Risen Christ, who is really present in the Sacrament of the Eucharist.

In the Gospel passage, St Luke mentions one of the appearances of the Risen Jesus (24: 35-48). At the very beginning of the passage the Evangelist notes that the two disciples of Emmaus, who hurried back to Jerusalem, had told the Eleven how they recognized him in "the breaking of the bread" (v. 35). And while they were recounting the extraordinary experience of their encounter with the Lord, he "himself stood among them" (v. 36). His sudden appearance frightened the Apostles. They were fearful to the point that Jesus, in order to reassure them and to overcome every hesitation and doubt, asked them to touch him – he was not a ghost but a man of flesh and bone – and then asked them for something to eat. Once again, as had happened for the two at Emmaus, it is at table while eating with his own that the Risen Christ reveals himself to the disciples, helping them to understand the Scriptures and to reinterpret the events of salvation in the light of Easter. "Everything written about me", he says, "in the law of Moses and the Prophets and the Psalms must be fulfilled" (v. 44). And he invites them to look to the future: "repentance and forgiveness of sins [shall] be preached in his name to all nations" (cf. v. 47).

This very experience of repentance and forgiveness is relived in every community in the Eucharistic Celebration, especially on Sundays. The Eucharist, the privileged place in which the Church recognizes "the Author of life" (Acts 3: 15) is "the breaking of the bread", as it is called in the Acts of the Apostles. In it, through faith, we enter into communion with Christ, who is "the priest, the altar, and the lamb of sacrifice" (cf. Easter Preface V) and is among us. Let us gather round him to cherish the memory of his words and of the events contained in Scripture; let us relive his Passion, death and Resurrection. In celebrating the Eucharist we communicate with Christ, the victim of expiation, and from him we draw forgiveness and life. What would our lives as Christians be without the Eucharist? The Eucharist is the perpetual, living inheritance which the Lord has bequeathed to us in the Sacrament of his Body and his Blood and which we must constantly rethink and deepen so that, as venerable Pope Paul VI said, it may "impress its inexhaustible effectiveness on all the days of our earthly life" (*Insegnamenti,* V [1967], p. 779). Nourished with the Eucharistic Bread, the Saints we are venerating today brought their mission of evangelical love to completion with their own special charisms in the various areas in which they worked.

St Arcangelo Tadini spent long hours in prayer before the Eucharist. Always focusing his pastoral ministry on the totality of the human person, he encouraged the human and spiritual growth of his parishioners. This holy priest, this holy parish priest, a man who belonged entirely to God ready in every circumstance to let himself be guided by the Holy Spirit, was at the same time prepared to face the urgent needs of the moment and find a remedy for them. For this reason he undertook many practical and courageous initiatives such as the organization of the "Catholic Workers Mutual Aid Association", the construction of a spinning mill and a residence for the workers and, in 1900, the foundation of the "Congregation of Worker Sisters of the Holy House of Nazareth" to evangelize the working world by sharing in the common efforts after the example of the Holy Family of Nazareth. How prophetic the charismatic intuition of Fr Tadini was and how timely his example remains today in an epoch of serious financial crisis! He reminds us that only by cultivating a constant and profound relationship with the Lord, especially in the Sacrament of the Eucharist, can we bring the Gospel leaven to the various fields of work and to every area of our society.

Love for prayer and for manual labour also distinguished St Bernardo Tolomei, the initiator of a unique Benedictine monastic movement. His was a Eucharistic life, entirely dedicated to contemplation, expressed in humble service to neighbour. Because of his rare spirit of humility and brotherly acceptance, he was re-elected abbot for 27 years, until his death. Moreover, in order to guarantee the future of his foundation, on 21 January 1344 he obtained from Clement VI papal approval of the new Benedictine Congregation called "Our Lady of Monte Oliveto". During the epidemic of the Black Death in 1348, he left the solitude of Monte Oliveto for the monastery of S. Benedetto at Porta Tufi, Siena, to attend to his monks stricken with the plague, and died, himself a victim, as an authentic martyr of love. The example of this Saint invites us to express our faith in a life dedicated to God in prayer and spent at the service of our neighbour, impelled by a love that is also ready to make the supreme sacrifice.

"Know that the Lord has set apart the godly for himself; the Lord hears when I call to him" (Ps 4: 3). These words of the Responsorial Psalm express the secret of the life of Bl. Nuno de Santa María, a hero and saint of Portugal. The 70 years of his life belong to the second half of the fourteenth century and the first half of the fifteenth, which saw this nation consolidate its independence from Castille and expand beyond the ocean not without a special plan of God opening new routes that were to favour the transit of Christ's Gospel to the ends of the earth. St Nuno felt he was an instrument of this lofty design and enrolled in the *militia Christi,* that is, in the service of witness that every Christian is called to bear in the world. He was characterized by an intense life of prayer and absolute trust in divine help.

Although he was an excellent soldier and a great leader, he never permitted these personal talents to prevail over the supreme action that comes from God. St Nuno allowed no obstacle to come in the way of God's action in his life, imitating Our Lady, to whom he was deeply devoted and to whom he publicly attributed his victories. At the end of his life, he retired to the Carmelite convent whose building he had commissioned. I am glad to point this exemplary figure out to the whole Church particularly because he exercised his life of faith and prayer in contexts apparently unfavourable to it, as proof that in any situation, even military or in war time, it is possible to act and to put into practice the values and principles of Christian life, especially if they are placed at the service of the common good and the glory of God.

Since childhood, Geltrude Comensoli felt a special attraction for Jesus present in the Eucharist. Adoration of Christ in the Eucharist became the principal aim of her life, we could almost say the habitual condition of her existence. Indeed, it was in the presence of the Eucharist that St Geltrude realized what her vocation and mission in the Church was to be: to dedicate herself without reserve to apostolic and missionary action, especially for youth. Thus, in obedience to Pope Leo XIII, her Institute came into being which endeavoured to translate the "charity contemplated" in the Eucharistic Christ, into "charity lived", in dedication to one's needy neighbour. In a bewildered and all too often wounded society like ours, to youth, like that of our day in search of values and a meaning for their lives, as a sound reference point St Geltrude points to God who, in the Eucharist, has made himself our travelling companion. She reminds us that "adoration must prevail over all the other charitable works", for it is from love for Christ who died and rose and who is really present in the Eucharistic Sacrament, that Gospel charity flows which impels us to see all human beings as our brothers and sisters.

St Caterina Volpicelli was also a witness of divine love. She strove "to belong to Christ in order to bring to Christ" those whom she met in Naples at the end of the nineteenth century, in a period of spiritual and social crisis. For her too the secret was the Eucharist. She recommended that her first collaborators cultivate an intense spiritual life in prayer and, especially, in vital contact with Jesus in the Eucharist. Today this is still the condition for continuing the work and mission which she began and which she bequeathed as a legacy to the "Servants of the Sacred Heart". In order to be authentic teachers of faith, desirous of passing on to the new generations the values of Christian culture, it is indispensable, as she liked to repeat, to release God from the prisons in which human beings have confined him. In fact, only in the Heart of Christ can humanity find its "permanent dwelling place". St Caterina shows to her spiritual daughters and to all of us the demanding journey of a conversion that radically changes the heart, and is expressed in actions consistent with the Gospel. It is thus possible to lay the foundations for building a society open to justice and solidarity, overcoming that economic and cultural imbalance which continues to exist in a large part of our planet.

Dear brothers and sisters, let us thank the Lord for the gift of holiness that shines out in the Church with rare beauty today in Arcangelo Tadini, Bernardo Tolomei, Nuno de Santa Maria Alvares Pereira, Geltrude Comensoli and Caterina Volpicelli. Let us be attracted by their examples, let us be guided by their teachings, so that our existence too may become a hymn of praise to God, in the footsteps of Jesus, worshipped with faith in the mystery of the Eucharist and served generously in our neighbour. May the maternal intercession of Mary, Queen of Saints and of these five new luminous examples of holiness whom we venerate joyfully today, obtain for us that we may carry out this evangelical mission. Amen!

Homily given during

HOLY MASS AND EUCHARISTIC PROCESSION TO THE BASILICA OF SAINT MARY MAJOR ON THE SOLEMNITY OF CORPUS CHRISTI

Square in front of the Basilica of Saint John Lateran
Thursday, 11 June 2009

'This is my Body . . . This is my Blood.'

These words that Jesus spoke at the Last Supper are repeated every time that the Eucharistic Sacrifice is renewed. We have just heard them in Mark's Gospel and they resonate with special power today on the Solemnity of Corpus Christi. They lead us in spirit to the Upper Room, they make us relive the spiritual atmosphere of that night when, celebrating Easter with his followers, the Lord mystically anticipated the sacrifice that was to be consummated the following day on the Cross. The Institution of the Eucharist thus appears to us as an anticipation and acceptance, on Jesus' part, of his death. St Ephrem the Syrian writes on this topic: during the Supper Jesus sacrificed himself; on the Cross he was sacrificed by others (cf. *Hymn on the Crucifixion*, 3, 1).

"This is my Blood". Here the reference to the sacrificial language of Israel is clear. Jesus presents himself as the true and definitive sacrifice, in which was fulfilled the expiation of sins which, in the Old Testament rites, was never fully completed. This is followed by two other very important remarks. First of all, Jesus Christ says that his Blood "is poured out for many" with a comprehensible reference to the songs of the Servant of God that are found in the Book of Isaiah (cf. ch. 53). With the addition "blood of the Covenant" Jesus also makes clear that through his death the prophecy of the new Covenant is fulfilled, based on the fidelity and infinite love of the Son made man. An alliance that, therefore, is stronger than all humanity's sins. The old Covenant had been sealed on Sinai with a sacrificial rite of animals, as we heard in the First Reading, and the Chosen People, set free from slavery in Egypt, had promised to obey all the commandments given to them by the Lord (cf. Ex 24: 3).

In truth, Israel showed immediately by making the golden calf that it was incapable of staying faithful to this promise and thus to the divine Covenant, which indeed it subsequently violated all too often, adapting to its heart of stone the Law that should have taught it the way of life. However, the Lord did not fail to keep his promise and, through the prophets, sought to recall the inner dimension of the Covenant and announced that he would write a new law upon the hearts of his faithful (cf. Jer 31: 33), transforming them with the gift of the Spirit (cf. Ez 36: 25-27). And it was during the Last Supper that he made this new Covenant with his disciples and humanity, confirming it not with animal sacrifices as had happened in the past, but indeed with his own Blood, which became the "Blood of the New Covenant". Thus he based it on his own obedience, stronger, as I said, than all our sins.

This is clearly highlighted in the Second Reading, taken from the Letter to the Hebrews, in which the sacred author declares that Jesus is the "mediator of a new covenant" (9:15). He became so through his blood, or, more exactly, through the gift of himself, which gives full value to the outpouring of his blood. On the Cross, Jesus is at the same time victim and priest: a victim worthy of God because he was unblemished, and a High Priest who offers himself, by the power of the Holy Spirit, and intercedes for the whole of humanity. The Cross is therefore a mystery of love and of salvation which cleanses us as the Letter to the Hebrews states from "dead works", that is, from sins, and sanctifies us by engraving the New Covenant upon our hearts. The Eucharist, making present the sacrifice of the Cross, renders us capable of living communion with God faithfully.

This evening let us too reaffirm our fidelity to the Lord. A few days ago, in opening the annual Diocesan Convention [of Rome], I recalled the importance of remaining, as Church, attentive to the word of God in prayer and in exploring the Scriptures, especially through the practice of *lectio divina*, that is, through reading the Bible in meditation and veneration. I know that in this respect many initiatives which enrich our diocesan community have been promoted in parishes, seminaries and religious communities, in confraternities and in apostolic associations and movements. I address my fraternal greeting to the members of this multiplicity of Church bodies. Your numerous presence at this celebration, dear friends, highlights the fact that God moulds our community, characterized by a plurality of cultures and by different experiences. God moulds it as "his" People, as the one Body of Christ, thanks to our heartfelt participation in the twofold banquet of the Word and of the Eucharist. Nourished by Christ, we, his disciples, receive the mission to be "the soul" of this City of ours (cf. *Letter to Diognetus,* 6: ed. Funk, I, p. 400; see also *Lumen Gentium* n. 38), a leaven of renewal, bread "broken" for all, especially for those in situations of hardship, poverty or physical and spiritual suffering. Let us become witnesses of his love.

I address you in particular, dear priests, whom Christ has

chosen so that with him you may be able to live your life as a sacrifice of praise for the salvation of the world. Only from union with Jesus can you draw that spiritual fruitfulness which generates hope in your pastoral ministry. St Leo the Great recalls that "our participation in the Body and Blood of Christ aspires to nothing other than to become what we receive" (*Sermo* 12, *De Passione* 3, 7, *PL* 54). If this is true for every Christian it is especially true for us priests. To become the Eucharist! May precisely this be our constant desire and commitment, so that the offering of the Body and Blood of the Lord which we make on the altar may be accompanied by the sacrifice of our existence. Every day, we draw from the Body and Blood of the Lord that free, pure love which makes us worthy ministers of Christ and witnesses to his joy. This is what the faithful expect of the priest: that is, the example of an authentic devotion to the Eucharist; they like to see him spend long periods of silence and adoration before Jesus as was the practice of the Holy Curé d'Ars, whom we shall remember in a special way during the upcoming Year for Priests.

St John Mary Vianney liked to tell his parishioners: "Come to communion. . . . It is true that you are not worthy of it, but you need it" (Bernard Nodet, *Le curé d'Ars. Sa pensée – Son coeur*, éd. Xavier Mappus, Paris 1995, p. 119). With the knowledge of being inadequate because of sin, but needful of nourishing ourselves with the love that the Lord offers us in the Eucharistic Sacrament, let us renew this evening our faith in the Real Presence of Christ in the Eucharist. We must not take this faith for granted! Today we run the risk of secularization creeping into the Church too. It can be translated into formal and empty Eucharistic worship, into celebrations lacking that heartfelt participation that is expressed in veneration and in respect for the liturgy. The temptation to reduce prayer to superficial, hasty moments, letting ourselves be overpowered by earthly activities and concerns, is always strong. When, in a little while, we recite the Our Father, the prayer *par excellence*, we will say: "Give us this day our daily bread", thinking of course of the bread of each day for us and for all peoples. But this request contains something deeper. The Greek word *epioúsios*, that we translate as "daily", could also allude to the "super-stantial" bread, the bread "of the world to come". Some Fathers of the Church saw this as a reference to the Eucharist, the bread of eternal life, the new world, that is already given to us in Holy Mass, so that from this moment the future world may begin within us. With the Eucharist, therefore, Heaven comes down to earth, the future of God enters the present and it is as though time were embraced by divine eternity.

Dear brothers and sisters, as happens every year, at the end of Holy Mass the traditional Eucharistic procession will set out and with prayer and hymns we shall raise a unanimous entreaty to the Lord present in the consecrated host. We shall say, on behalf of the entire city: "Stay with us Jesus, make a gift of yourself and give us the bread that nourishes us for eternal life! Free this world from the poison of evil, violence and hatred that pollute consciences, purify it with the power of your merciful love." "And you, Mary, who were the woman 'of the Eucharist' throughout your life, help us to walk united towards the heavenly goal, nourished by the Body and Blood of Christ, the eternal Bread of life and medicine of divine immortality." Amen!

II
ADDRESSES

ANGELUS

Saint Peter's Square
Sunday, 18 June 2006

'The "Treasure" of the Church'

Today, in Italy and in other countries, the Solemnity of Corpus Christi is celebrated, which already had its intense moment in Rome in the city's procession on Thursday. It is the solemn, public feast of the Eucharist, the Sacrament of the Body and Blood of Christ: on this day, the mystery instituted at the Last Supper and commemorated every year on Holy Thursday is manifested to all, in the midst of the fervour of faith and devotion of the Ecclesial Community. Indeed, the Eucharist is the "treasure" of the Church, the precious heritage that her Lord has left to her. And the Church preserves it with the greatest care, celebrating it daily in Holy Mass, adoring it in churches and chapels, administering it to the sick, and as viaticum to those who are on their last journey.

However, this treasure that is destined for the baptized, does not exhaust its radius of action in the context of the Church: the Eucharist is the Lord Jesus who gives himself "for the life of the world" (Jn 6: 51). In every time and in every place, he wants to meet human beings and bring them the life of God. And this is not all. The Eucharist also has a cosmic property: the transformation of the bread and the wine into Christ's Body and Blood is in fact the principle of the divinization of creation itself.

For this reason, the Feast of Corpus Christi is characterized particularly by the tradition of carrying the Most Holy

Sacrament in procession, an act full of meaning. By carrying the Eucharist through the streets and squares, we desire to immerse the Bread come down from Heaven in our daily lives. We want Jesus to walk where we walk, to live where we live. Our world, our existence, must become his temple. On this feast day, the Christian Community proclaims that the Eucharist is its all, its very life, the source of life that triumphs over death. From communion with Christ in the Eucharist flows the charity that transforms our life and supports us all on our journey towards the heavenly Homeland. For this reason the liturgy makes us sing "Good Shepherd, true Bread. . . . You who know all things, who can do all things, who nourish us while on earth, lead your brethren to the heavenly banquet in the glory of your Saints."

Mary is the "Woman of the Eucharist" as Pope John Paul II described her in his Encyclical *Ecclesia de Eucharistia*. Let us pray the Virgin that all Christians may deepen their faith in the Eucharistic mystery, to live in constant communion with Jesus and be his effective witness.

ANGELUS

Saint Peter's Square
Sunday, 10 June 2007

Adoration

Today's Solemnity of Corpus Christi, which was celebrated last Thursday in the Vatican and in different nations, invites us to contemplate the supreme Mystery of our faith: the Most Holy Eucharist, the Real Presence of the Lord Jesus Christ in the Sacrament of the Altar. Every time that the priest renews the Eucharistic Sacrifice, in the prayer of consecration he repeats: "This is my Body . . . this is my Blood."

He says this lending his voice, hands and heart to Christ, who wanted to stay with us and be the heartbeat of the Church. However, after the celebration of the divine Mysteries, the Lord Jesus remains alive in the tabernacle; for this reason special praise is given to him with Eucharistic adoration, as I wished to recall in the recent Post-Synodal Apostolic Exhortation *Sacramentum Caritatis* (cf. nn. 66-69).

Indeed, an intrinsic connection exists between celebration and adoration. In fact, Holy Mass is in itself the Church's greatest act of adoration: "No one eats of this flesh", as St Augustine writes, "without having first adored it" (*Enarr. in Ps. 98,9: CCL* XXXIX, 1385).

Adoration outside Holy Mass prolongs and intensifies what has taken place in the liturgical celebration and makes a true and profound reception of Christ possible.

Today, then, the Eucharistic procession is taking place in Christian communities in all parts of the world. It is a special form of public adoration of the Eucharist, enriched by beautiful and traditional expressions of popular devotion. I would like to take the opportunity offered to me by today's Solemnity to warmly recommend, to Pastors and to all the faithful, the practice of Eucharistic adoration.

I express my appreciation to the Institutes of Consecrated Life as well as to the associations and confraternities that are especially dedicated to this practice; they offer to everyone a reminder of Christ's centrality in our personal and ecclesial life.

Then I rejoice to see that many young people are discovering the beauty of adoration, both privately and in groups. I ask priests to encourage these youth groups in their adoration, but also to guide them, to ensure that the form of their community adoration is always appropriate and dignified and that they allow sufficient time for silence and listening to the Word of God.

In life today, often noisy and distracted, it is more important than ever to recover the capacity for inner silence and recollection. Eucharistic adoration permits this not only centred on the "I" but more so in the company of that "You" full of love who is Jesus Christ, "the God who is near to us".

May the Virgin Mary, the Woman of the Eucharist, introduce us into the secret of true adoration. Her humble and simple heart was ever pondering the mystery of Jesus, in whom she adored the presence of God and of his redeeming love. May faith in the Eucharistic Mystery, joy in participating in Holy Mass, especially on Sundays, and enthusiasm in witnessing to Christ's immense love grow throughout the Church through her intercession.

ANGELUS

St Peter's Square
Sunday, 25 May 2008

'School of Charity'

Today in Italy and in various countries is the Solemnity of Corpus Christi, which in the Vatican and in other nations was celebrated last Thursday. It is the feast of the Eucharist, wonderful gift of Christ, who at the Last Supper wanted to leave us the memorial of his Pasch, the Sacrament of his Body and of his Blood, a pledge of his immense love for us. A week ago our gaze was drawn to the mystery of the Most Holy Trinity. Today we are invited to fix our gaze on the consecrated Host: it is the same God! The same Love! This is the beauty of the Christian truth: the Creator and Lord of all things makes himself a "grain of wheat" to be sown in our land, in the furrows of our history. He made himself bread to be broken, shared, eaten. He made himself our food to give us life, his same divine life. He was born in Bethlehem, which in Hebrew means "House of bread", and when he began to preach to the crowds he revealed that the Father had sent him into the world as "living bread come down from heaven", as the "bread of life".

The Eucharist is a school of charity and solidarity. The one who is nourished on the Bread of Christ cannot remain indifferent before the one who, even in our day, is deprived of daily bread. So many parents are barely able to obtain it for themselves and for their own children. It is an ever greater problem that the International Community has great difficulty in resolving. The Church not only prays "give us this day our daily bread", but, on the Lord's example, is committed in every way to "multiply the five loaves and the two fish" with numerous initiatives of human promotion and sharing, so that no one lacks what is necessary for life.

Dear brothers and sisters, the feast of Corpus Christi is an occasion to grow in this concrete attention to our brethren, especially the poor. May the Virgin Mary obtain this grace for us, from whom the Son of God took flesh and blood, as we repeat in a famous Eucharistic hymn, set to music by several great composers: *"Ave verum corpus natum de Maria Virgine"*, and which concludes with the invocation: *"O Iesu dulcis, o Iesu pie, o Iesu fili Mariae!"* May Mary, who bearing Jesus in her womb was the first living "tabernacle" of the Eucharist, communicate to us her same faith in the holy mystery of the Body and Blood of her divine Son, so that it may truly be the centre of our life.

APOSTOLIC JOURNEY OF HIS HOLINESS
BENEDICT XVI TO FRANCE ON THE
OCCASION OF THE 150th ANNIVERSARY
OF THE APPARITIONS OF THE BLESSED
VIRGIN MARY AT LOURDES
12-15 SEPTEMBER 2008

BLESSED SACRAMENT PROCESSION

Prairie, Lourdes
Sunday, 14 September 2008

Meditation

Lord Jesus, You are here!
  And you, my brothers, my sisters, my friends,
  You are here, with me, in his presence!
  Lord, two thousand years ago, you willingly mounted the infamous Cross in order then to rise again and to remain for ever with us, your brothers and sisters.
  And you, my brothers, my sisters, my friends,
  You willingly allow him to embrace you.
  We contemplate him.
  We adore him.
  We love him. We seek to grow in love for him.
  We contemplate him who, in the course of his Passover meal, gave his Body and Blood to his disciples, so as to be with them "always, to the close of the age" (Mt 28: 20).

We adore him who is the origin and goal of our faith, him without whom we would not be here this evening, without whom we would not be at all, without whom there would be nothing, absolutely nothing! Him through whom "all things were made" (Jn 1: 3), him in whom we were created, for all eternity, him who gave us his own Body and Blood – he is here, this evening, in our midst, for us to gaze upon.

We love, and we seek to grow in love for him who is here, in our presence, for us to gaze upon, for us perhaps to question, for us to love.

Whether we are walking or nailed to a bed of suffering; whether we are walking in joy or languishing in the wilderness of the soul (cf. Num 21: 4): Lord, take us all into your Love; the infinite Love which is eternally the Love of the Father for the Son and the Son for the Father, the Love of the Father and the Son for the Spirit, and the Love of the Spirit for the Father and the Son. The Sacred Host exposed to our view speaks of this infinite power of Love manifested on the glorious Cross. The Sacred Host speaks to us of the incredible abasement of the One who made himself poor so as to make us rich in him, the One who accepted the loss of everything so as to win us for his Father. The Sacred Host is the living, efficacious and real Sacrament of the eternal presence of the Saviour of mankind to his Church.

My brothers, my sisters, my friends,

Let us accept; may you accept to offer yourselves to him who has given us everything, who came not to judge the world, but to save it (cf. Jn 3: 17), accept to recognize in your lives the presence of him who is present here, exposed to our view. Accept to offer him your very lives!

Mary, the holy Virgin, Mary, the Immaculate Conception, accepted, two thousand years ago, to give everything, to offer her body so as to receive the Body of the Creator. Everything came from Christ, even Mary; everything came through Mary, even Christ.

Mary, the holy Virgin, is with us this evening, in the presence of the Body of her Son, one hundred and fifty years after revealing herself to little Bernadette.

Holy Virgin, help us to contemplate, help us to adore, help us to love, to grow in love for him who loved us so much, so as to live eternally with him.

An immense crowd of witnesses is invisibly present beside us, very close to this blessed grotto and in front of this church that the Virgin Mary wanted to be built; the crowd of all those men and women who have contemplated, venerated, adored the Real Presence of him who gave himself to us even to the last drop of blood; the crowd of all those men and women who have spent hours in adoration of the Most Holy Sacrament of the altar.

This evening, we do not see them, but we hear them saying to us, to every man and to every woman among us: "Come, let the Master call you! He is here! He is calling you (cf. Jn 11: 28)! He wants to take your life and join it to his. Let yourself be embraced by him! Gaze no longer upon your own wounds, gaze upon his. Do not look upon what still separates you from him and from others; look upon the infinite distance that he has abolished by taking your flesh, by mounting the Cross which men had prepared for him, and by letting himself be put to death so as to show you his love. In his wounds, he takes hold of you; in his wounds, he hides you. Do not refuse his Love!"

The immense crowd of witnesses who have allowed themselves to be embraced by his Love, is the crowd of saints in heaven who never cease to intercede for us. They were sinners and they knew it, but they willingly ceased to gaze upon their own wounds and to gaze only upon the wounds of their Lord, so as to discover there the glory of the Cross, to discover there the victory of Life over death. Saint Pierre-Julien Eymard tells us everything when he cries out: "The holy Eucharist is Jesus Christ, past, present and future" (*Sermons and Parochial Instructions after 1856*, 4-2.1, 'On Meditation').

Jesus Christ, past, in the historical truth of the evening in the Upper Room, to which every celebration of holy Mass leads us back.

Jesus Christ, present, because he said to us: "Take and eat of this, all of you, this is my body, this is my blood." "This is", in the present, here and now, as in every here and now throughout human history. The Real Presence, the presence which surpasses our poor lips, our poor hearts, our poor thoughts. The presence offered for us to gaze upon as we do here, this evening, close to the grotto where Mary revealed herself as the Immaculate Conception.

The Eucharist is also Jesus Christ, future, Jesus Christ to come. When we contemplate the Sacred Host, his glorious transfigured and risen Body, we contemplate what we shall contemplate in eternity, where we shall discover that the whole world has been carried by its Creator during every second of its history. Each time we consume him, but also each time we contemplate him, we proclaim him until he comes again, "*donec veniat*". That is why we receive him with infinite respect.

Some of us cannot – or cannot yet – receive Him in the Sacrament, but we can contemplate Him with faith and love and express our desire finally to be united with Him. This desire has great value in God's presence: such people await his return more ardently; they await Jesus Christ who must come again.

When, on the day after her First Communion, a friend of Bernadette asked her: "What made you happier: your First Communion or the apparitions?", Bernadette replied, "they are two things that go together, but cannot be compared. I was happy in both" (*Emmanuélite Estrade*, 4 June 1958). She made this testimony to the Bishop of Tarbes in regard to her First

Communion: "Bernadette behaved with immense concentration, with an attention that left nothing to be desired . . . she appeared profoundly aware of the holy action that was taking place. Everything developed in her in an astonishing way."

With Pierre-Julien Eymard and Bernadette, we invoke the witness of countless men and women saints who had the greatest love for the holy Eucharist. Nicolas Cabasilas cries out to us this evening: "If Christ dwells within us, what do we need? What do we lack? If we dwell in Christ, what more could we desire? He is our host and our dwelling-place. Happy are we to be his home! What joy to be ourselves the dwelling-place of such an inhabitant!"

Blessed Charles de Foucauld was born in 1858, the very year of the apparitions at Lourdes. Not far from his body, stiffened by death, there lay, like the grain of wheat cast upon the earth, the lunette containing the Blessed Sacrament which Brother Charles adored every day for many a long hour. Father de Foucauld has given us a prayer from the depths of his heart, a prayer addressed to our Father, but one which, with Jesus, we can in all truth make our own in the presence of the sacred host:

'Father, into your hands I commend my spirit.'

This was the last prayer of our Master, our Beloved. . . . May it also be our own prayer, and not only at our last moment, but at every moment in our lives: Father, I commit myself into your hands; Father, I trust in you; Father, I abandon myself to you; Father, do with me what you will; whatever you may do, I thank you; thank you for everything; I am ready for all, I accept all; I thank you for all. Let only your will be done in me, Lord, let only your will be done in all your creatures, in all your children, in all those whom your heart loves, I wish no more than this, O Lord. Into your hands I commend my soul; I offer it to you, Lord, with all the love of my heart, for I love you, and so need to give myself in love, to surrender myself into your hands, without reserve, and with boundless confidence, for you are my Father.

Beloved brothers and sisters, day pilgrims and inhabitants of these valleys, brother bishops, priests, deacons, men and women religious, all of you who see before you the infinite abasement of the Son of God and the infinite glory of the Resurrection, remain in silent adoration of your Lord, our Master and Lord Jesus Christ. Remain silent, then speak and tell the world: we cannot be silent about what we know. Go and tell the whole world the marvels of God, present at every moment of our lives, in every place on earth. May God bless us and keep us, may he lead us on the path of eternal life, he who is Life, for ever and ever. Amen.

GENERAL AUDIENCE

St Peter's Square
Wednesday, 15 October 2008

The Body of Christ

The Paschal Mystery, which brought the Apostle to the turning point in his life on the road to Damascus, obviously lies at the heart of his preaching (1 Cor 2: 2; 15: 14). This Mystery, proclaimed in the Word, is brought about in the Sacraments of Baptism and of the Eucharist and then becomes reality in Christian love. Paul's only goal in his work of evangelization is to establish the community of believers in Christ. This idea is inherent in the actual etymology of the term *ekklesia,* which Paul, and with him all Christendom, preferred to the term "synagogue": not only because the former is originally more "secular" (deriving from the Greek practice of the political assembly which was not exactly religious), but also because it directly involves the more theological idea of a call *ab extra,* and is not, therefore, a mere gathering; believers are called by God, who gathers them in a community, his Church.

Along these lines we can also understand the original concept, exclusively Pauline, of the Church as the "Body of Christ". In this regard it is necessary to bear in mind the two dimensions of this concept. One is sociological in character, according to which the body is made up of its elements and would not exist without them. This interpretation appears in the Letter to the Romans and in the First Letter to the Corinthians, in which Paul uses an image that already existed in Roman sociology: he says that a people is like a body with its different parts, each of which has its own function but all together, even its smallest and seemingly most insignificant parts, are necessary if this body is to be able to live and carry out its functions. The Apostle appropriately observes that in the Church there are many vocations: prophets, apostles, teachers, simple people, all are called to practise charity every day, all are necessary in order to build the living unity of this spiritual organism. The other interpretation refers to the actual Body of Christ. Paul holds that the Church is not only an organism but really becomes the Body of Christ in the Sacrament of the Eucharist, where we all receive his Body and really become his Body. Thus is brought about the spousal mystery that all become one body and one spirit in Christ. So it is that the reality goes far beyond any sociological image, expressing its real, profound essence, that is, the oneness of all the baptized in Christ, considered by the Apostle "one" in Christ, conformed to the Sacrament of his Body.

In saying this, Paul shows that he knows well and makes us all understand that the Church is not his and is not ours: the Church is the Body of Christ, it is a "Church *of God*", "God's field, God's building . . . God's temple" (1 Cor 3: 9, 16). This latter designation is particularly interesting because it attributes to a fabric of interpersonal relations a term that commonly served to mean a physical place, considered sacred. The relationship between church and temple therefore comes to assume two complementary dimensions: on the one hand the characteristic of separateness and purity that the sacred building deserved is applied to the ecclesial community, but on the other, the concept of a material space is also overcome, to transfer this quality to the reality of a living community of faith. If previously temples had been considered places of God's presence, it was now known and seen that God does not dwell in buildings made of stone but that the place of God's presence in the world is the living community of believers.

GENERAL AUDIENCE

Paul VI Audience Hall
Wednesday, 10 December 2008

'Christ gives us Himself'

We now come to the Sacrament of the Eucharist. I have already shown in other Catecheses the profound respect with which St Paul transmits verbally the tradition of the Eucharist which he received from the witnesses of the last night themselves. He passes on these words as a precious treasure entrusted to his fidelity. Thus we really hear in these words the witnesses of the last night. We heard the words of the Apostle: "For I received from the Lord what I also delivered to you, that the Lord Jesus on the night when he was betrayed took bread, and when he had given thanks, he broke it, and said, 'This is my Body which is for you. Do this in remembrance of me.' In the same way also the cup, after supper, saying, 'This cup is the new covenant in my Blood. Do this, as often as you drink it, in remembrance of me'" (1 Cor 11: 23-35). It is an inexhaustible text. Here too, in this Catechesis, I have only two brief remarks to make. Paul transmits the Lord's words over the cup like this: this cup is "the new covenant in my Blood". These words conceal an allusion to two fundamental texts of the Old Testament. The first refers to the promise of a new covenant in the Book of the Prophet Jeremiah. Jesus tells the disciples and tells us: now, at this moment, with me and with my death the new covenant is fulfilled; by my Blood this new history of humanity begins in the world. However, also present in these words is a reference to the moment of the covenant on Sinai, when Moses said: "Behold the blood of the covenant which the Lord has made with you in accordance with all these words" (Ex 24: 8). Then it was the blood of animals. The blood of animals could only be the expression of a desire, an expectation of the true sacrifice, the true worship. With the gift of the cup, the Lord gives us the true sacrifice. The one true sacrifice is the love of the Son. With the gift of this love, eternal love, the world enters into the new covenant. Celebrating the Eucharist means that Christ gives us himself, his love, to configure us to himself and thereby to create the new world.

The second important aspect of the teaching on the Eucharist appears in the same First Letter to the Corinthians where St Paul says: "the cup of blessing which we bless, is it not a participation in the Blood of Christ? The bread which we break, is it not a participation in the Body of Christ? Because there is one bread, we who are many are one body, for we all partake of the one bread" (10: 16-17). In these words the personal and social character of the Sacrament of the Eucharist likewise appears. Christ personally unites himself with each one of us, but Christ himself is also united with the man and the woman who are next to me. And the bread is for me but it is also for the other. Thus Christ unites all of us with himself and all of us with one another. In communion we receive Christ. But Christ is likewise united with my neighbour: Christ and my neighbour are inseparable in the Eucharist. And thus we are all one bread and one body. A Eucharist without solidarity with others is a Eucharist abused. And here we come to the root and, at the same time, the kernel of the doctrine on the Church as the Body of Christ, of the Risen Christ.

We also perceive the full realism of this doctrine. Christ gives us his Body in the Eucharist, he gives himself in his Body and thus makes us his Body, he unites us with his Risen Body. If man eats ordinary bread, in the digestive process this bread becomes part of his body, transformed into a substance of human life. But in Holy Communion the inverse process is brought about. Christ, the Lord, assimilates us into himself, introducing us into his glorious Body, and thus we all become his Body. Whoever reads only chapter 12 of the First Letter to the Corinthians and chapter 12 of the Letter to the Romans might think that the words about the Body of Christ as an organism of charisms is only a sort of sociological and theological parable. Actually in Roman political science this parable of the body with various members that form a single unit was used referring to the State itself, to say that the State is an organism in which each one has his role, that the multiplicity and diversity of functions form one body and each one has his place. If one reads only chapter 12 of the First Letter to the Corinthians one might think that Paul limited himself to transferring this alone to the Church, that here too it was solely a question of a sociology of the Church. Yet, bearing in mind this chapter 10, we see that the realism of the Church is something quite different, far deeper and truer than that of a State organism. Because Christ really gives his Body and makes us his Body. We really become united with the Risen Body of Christ and thereby are united with one another. The Church is not only a corporation like the State is, she is a body. She is not merely an organization but a real organism.

TO PARTICIPANTS IN THE PLENARY ASSEMBLY OF THE CONGREGATION FOR DIVINE WORSHIP AND THE DISCIPLINE OF THE SACRAMENTS

Consistory Hall
Friday, 13 March 2009

'Worship must become union'

The Second Vatican Council shed light on the unique role that the Eucharistic mystery plays in the life of the faithful (*Sacrosanctum Concilium*, nn. 48-54, 56). As Pope Paul VI said on various occasions: "the Eucharist is a very great mystery, in fact, properly speaking and in the words of the Sacred Liturgy, the *mystery of faith*" (*Mysterium Fidei,* n. 15). In fact, the Eucharist is present at the Church's very origins (cf. John Paul II, *Ecclesia de Eucharistia,* n. 21) and is the source of grace that constitutes an incomparable opportunity both for the sanctification of humanity in Christ and for the glorification of God. In this sense, on the one hand all the Church's activities are ordained to the mystery of the Eucharist (cf. *Sacrosanctum Concilium,* n. 10; *Lumen Gentium,* n. 11; *Presbyterorum Ordinis,* n. 5; *Sacramentum Caritatis,* n. 17) and, moreover, it is by virtue of the Eucharist that "the Church ever derives her life and on which she thrives" (*Lumen*

Gentium, n. 26), today too. Our task is to perceive the most precious treasure of this ineffable mystery of faith "not only in the celebration of Mass but also in devotion to the sacred species which remain after Mass and are reserved to extend the grace of the sacrifice" (Instruction *Eucharisticum mysterium,* n. 3, g). The doctrine of the transubstantiation of the bread and the wine and of the Real Presence are truths of faith that are also visible in Sacred Scripture itself and were subsequently confirmed by the Fathers of the Church. In this regard, Pope Paul VI recalled that "the Catholic Church has held firm to this belief in the presence of Christ's Body and Blood in the Eucharist not only in her teaching but in her life as well, since she has at all times paid this great Sacrament the worship known as 'latria' which may be given to God alone" (*Mysterium Fidei,* n. 55; cf. *Catechism of the Catholic Church,* n. 1378).

It is appropriate to remember in this regard the different meanings of the word "adoration" in the Greek and Latin languages. The Greek word *proskýnesis* means the act of submission, the recognition of God as our true measure and by whose law we agree to abide. The Latin word *adoratio,* on the other hand, denotes the physical contact, the kiss, the embrace, which is implicit in the idea of love. The aspect of submission foresees a relationship of union because the one to whom we submit is Love. Indeed, in the Eucharist, worship must become union: union with the living Lord and then with his Mystical Body. As I said to the young people on the Marienfeld Esplanade during the 20th World Youth Day in Cologne on 21 August 2005, "God no longer simply stands before us as the One who is totally Other. He is within us, and we are in him. His dynamic enters into us and then seeks to spread outwards to others until it fills the world, so that his love can truly become the dominant measure of the world" (Mass for the conclusion of the World Youth Day, Cologne). In this perspective I reminded the young people that in the Eucharist one lives the "fundamental transformation of violence into love, of death into life, [which] brings other changes in its wake. Bread and wine become his Body and Blood. But it must not stop there; on the contrary, the process of transformation must now gather momentum. The Body and Blood of Christ are given to us so that we ourselves will be transformed in our turn" (ibid.).

In his Apostolic Letter *Spiritus et Sponsa* on the occasion of the 40th anniversary of the Constitution *Sacrosanctum Concilium* on the Sacred Liturgy, my Predecessor Pope John Paul II urged the faithful to take the necessary steps to deepen their experience of renewal. This is also important concerning the topic of Eucharistic adoration. This deepening will only be possible through greater knowledge of the mystery in total fidelity to sacred Tradition and increasing liturgical life within our communities (cf. *Spiritus et Sponsa,* 4 December 2003, nn. 6-7). In this regard I particularly appreciate the fact that the Plenary Assembly also reflected on the subject of the formation in the faith of the whole People of God with special attention to seminarians, in order to increase growth in a spirit of authentic Eucharistic adoration. In fact, St Thomas explains "that in this sacrament are the true Body of Christ and his true Blood is something that "cannot be apprehended by the senses' but only by faith, which relies on divine authority" (*Summa Theologiae,* III, 75, 1; cf. *Catechism of the Catholic Church,* n. 1381).

GENERAL AUDIENCE

Saint Peter's Square
Wednesday, 8 April 2009

'In the Upper Room'

In the afternoon Mass, called *in Coena Domini,* the Church commemorates the institution of the Eucharist, the ministerial priesthood and the new Commandment of love that Jesus entrusted to his disciples. St Paul offers one of the oldest accounts of what happened in the Upper Room, on the vigil of the Lord's Passion. "The Lord Jesus", he writes at the beginning of the 50s, on the basis of a text he received from the Lord's own followers, "on the night in which he was betrayed took bread, and after he had given thanks, broke it and said, 'This is my body, which is for you. Do this in remembrance of me'. In the same way, after the supper, he took the cup, saying, 'This cup is the new covenant in my blood. Do this, whenever you drink it, in remembrance of me'" (1 Cor 11: 23-25). These words, laden with mystery, clearly show Christ's will: under the species of the Bread and the Wine, he makes himself present with his Body given and his Blood poured out. This is the sacrifice of the new and everlasting covenant offered to all, without distinction of race or culture. It is from this sacramental rite, which he presents to the Church as the supreme evidence of his love, that Jesus makes ministers of his disciples and all those who will continue the ministry through the centuries. Thus, Holy Thursday constitutes a renewed invitation to give thanks to God for the supreme gift of the Eucharist, to receive with devotion and to adore with living faith. For this reason the Church encourages the faithful to keep vigil in the presence of the Blessed Sacrament after the celebration of Holy Mass, recalling the sorrowful hour that Jesus spent in solitude and prayer at Gethsemane, before being arrested and then sentenced to death.

ANGELUS

St Peter's Square
Sunday, 14 June 2009

'Love transforms all things'

Corpus Christi, the feast of the Eucharist in which the Sacrament of the Body of the Lord is solemnly carried in procession, is being celebrated today in various countries, including Italy. What does this feastday mean to us? It does not make us think of the liturgical aspect alone; actually Corpus Christi is a day that involves the cosmic dimension, the heavens and the earth. It calls to mind first of all at least in our hemisphere this season which is so beautiful and fragrant, in which Spring is already turning into Summer, the sun is high in the sky and the wheat is ripening in the fields. The Church's feasts like the Jewish feasts are associated with the phases of the solar year, the sowing and the reaping. This is particularly evident in today's Solemnity, at the heart of which is the sign of bread, a fruit of the earth and of Heaven. The Eucharistic Bread is thus a visible sign of the One in whom Heaven and earth, God and man, became one. And this shows that the relationship with the seasons is not something merely external to the liturgical year.

The Solemnity of Corpus Christi is closely linked to Easter and Pentecost: the death and Resurrection of Jesus and the outpouring of the Holy Spirit are its premises. Furthermore, it is directly linked to the Feast of the Trinity that was celebrated last Sunday. It is only because God himself is relationship that there can be a relationship with him; and only because he is love can he love and be loved. Thus, Corpus Christi is a manifestation of

God, an attestation that God is love. This feast speak
unique and special way of divine love, of what it is an
does. It tells us, for example, that it is regenerated in self-giving,
that it is received in self-giving, that it is never lacking nor can
it be consumed as a hymn by St Thomas Aquinas sings: *"nec
sumptus consumitur"*. Love transforms all things and we therefore
understand that the centre of today's Feast of Corpus Christi is
the mystery of transubstantiation, a sign of Jesus Christ who
transforms the world. Looking at him and worshipping him,
we say: "yes, love exists and because it exists things can change
for the better and we can hope." It is hope that comes from
Christ's love which gives us the strength to live and to deal with
difficulties. For this reason let us sing as we carry the Most Holy
Sacrament in procession; let us sing and praise God who revealed
himself concealing himself in the sign of the Bread broken. We
are all in need of this Bread, as the journey to freedom, justice
and peace is long and difficult.

We can imagine with what great faith and love Our Lady must
have received and adored the Blessed Eucharist in her heart! For
her it must have been every time like reliving the whole mystery
of her Son Jesus: from his Conception to his Resurrection.
The "Woman of the Eucharist", my venerable and beloved
Predecessor John Paul II called her. Let us learn from her to
renew our communion with the Body of Christ ceaselessly so
that we may love one another as he loved us.

From the Homily given at

VESPERS ON THE OCCASION OF THE REOPENING OF THE RESTORED PAULINE CHAPEL IN THE VATICAN APOSTOLIC PALACE

Pauline Chapel
Saturday, 4 July 2009

'The whole work of Redemption'

The Eucharist is the Sacrament in which the whole work of Redemption is concentrated: in Jesus as Eucharist we can contemplate the transformation of death into life, of violence into love. Hidden beneath the veils of the bread and the wine, we recognize through the eyes of faith the same glory that was manifested to the Apostles after the Resurrection. It is the same glory that Peter, James and John contemplated as a foretaste on the mountain, when Jesus was transfigured before them: a mysterious event, the Transfiguration, which the large painting in this chapel by Simone Cantarini presents anew with unique force. In fact, however, the entire chapel, the frescoes of Lorenzo Sabatini and Federico Zuccari, the decorations of numerous other artists brought here on another occasion by Pope Gregory XIII, all of it flows together into a single, unique hymn of the triumph of life and grace over death and sin, in a symphony of worship and of love for Christ the Redeemer that is highly evocative.

ANGELUS

St Peter's Square
Sunday, 5 July 2009

The Most Precious Blood

The first Sunday of July was formerly marked by the devotion to the Most Precious Blood of Christ. Several of my venerable Predecessors confirmed this in the past century and Bl. John XXIII, with his Apostolic Letter *Inde a Primis* (30 June 1960), explained its meaning and approved its Litanies. The theme of blood, linked to that of the Paschal Lamb, is of primary importance in Sacred Scripture. In the Old Testament, aspersion with the blood of sacrificed animals represented and established the covenant between God and his People, as we read in the Book of Exodus: "and Moses took the blood and threw it upon the people, and said, 'Behold the blood of the covenant which the Lord has made with you in accordance with all these words'" (Ex 24: 8).

Jesus refers explicitly to this formula during the Last Supper, when, offering the cup to the disciples, he says: "This is my blood of the covenant, which is poured out for many for the forgiveness of sins" (Mt 26: 28). And effectively, from the scourging to the piercing of his side after his death on the Cross, Christ poured out all his Blood as the true Lamb sacrificed for the redemption of all. The salvific value of his Blood is expressly stated in many passages of the New Testament. It suffices to mention, in this Year for Priests, the beautiful words of the Letter to the Hebrews: "Christ . . . entered once for all into the Holy Place, taking not the blood of goats and calves but his own Blood, thus securing an eternal redemption. For if the sprinkling of defiled persons with the blood of goats and bulls and with the ashes of a heifer sanctifies for the purification of the flesh, how much more shall the Blood of Christ, who through the eternal Spirit offered himself without blemish to God, purify your conscience from dead works to serve the living God" (9: 11-14).

Dear Brothers, it is written in Genesis that the blood of Abel, killed by his brother Caine, cries to God from the earth (cf. 4: 10). And, unfortunately, today as in the past, this cry never ceases, as human blood continues to be shed because of violence, injustice and hatred. When will human beings learn that life is sacred and belongs to God alone? When will they understand that we are all brothers and sisters? To the cry which rises from so many parts of the earth for the blood that is spilled, God responds with the Blood of his Son, who gave his life for us. Christ did not respond to evil with evil but with goodness, with his infinite love. The Blood of Christ is the pledge of God's faithful love for humanity. Every human being, even in conditions of extreme moral wretchedness can say, fixing his eyes on the wounds of the Crucified One: "God has not abandoned me, he loves me, he has given his life for me", and thus rediscover hope. May the Virgin Mary, who at the foot of the Cross together with the Apostle John received the testament of Jesus' Blood, help us to rediscover the inestimable richness of this grace and to feel deep and everlasting gratitude for it.

From the

ANGELUS

Les Combes (Val D'Aosta)
Sunday, 26 July 2009

The Miracle of the Loaves

Today, on this splendid Sunday, as the Lord shows us all the beauty of his Creation, the liturgy provides us with the Gospel passage at the beginning of Chapter Six of John's Gospel. It contains, first of all, the miracle of the loaves – when Jesus fed thousands of people with only five loaves of bread and two fish; then, the Lord's miracle when he walks on the waters of the lake during a storm; and finally, the discourse in which he reveals himself as "the Bread of Life". In recounting the "sign" of bread, the Evangelist emphasizes that Christ, before distributing the food, blessed it with a prayer of thanksgiving (cf. v. 11). The Greek term used is *eucharistein* and it refers directly to the Last Supper, though, in fact, John refers here not to the institution of the Eucharist but to the washing of the feet. The Eucharist is mentioned here in anticipation of the great symbol of the Bread of Life. In this Year for Priests, how can we fail to recall that we priests, especially, may see ourselves reflected in this Johannine text, identifying ourselves with the Apostles when they say: Where can we find bread for all these people? Reading about that unknown boy who has five barley loaves and two fish, we too spontaneously say: But what are they for such a multitude? In other words: Who am I? How can I, with my limitations, help Jesus in his mission? And the Lord gives the answer: By taking in his "holy and venerable" hands the little that they are, priests, we priests, become instruments of salvation for many, for everyone!

ANGELUS

Courtyard of the Papal Summer Residence,
Castel Gandolfo
Sunday, 16 August 2009

'I am the Living Bread'

Yesterday we celebrated the great Feast of Mary taken up into Heaven, and today we read these words of Jesus in the Gospel: "I am the living bread which came down from heaven" (Jn 6: 51). One cannot but be struck by this parallel that rotates around the symbol of "Heaven": Mary was "taken up" to the very place from which her Son had "come down". Of course, this language, which is biblical, expresses in figurative terms something that never completely coincides with the world of our own concepts and images. But let us pause for a moment to think! Jesus presents himself as the "living bread", that is, the food which contains the life of God itself which it can communicate to those who eat it, the true nourishment that gives life, which is really and deeply nourishing. Jesus says: "if any one eats of this bread, he will live for ever; and the bread which I shall give for the life of the world is my flesh" (Jn 6: 51). Well, *from whom* did the Son of God take his "flesh", his actual, earthly humanity? He took it from the Virgin Mary. In order to enter our mortal condition, God took from her a human body. In turn, at the end of her earthly life, the Virgin's body was taken up into Heaven by God and brought to enter the heavenly condition. It is a sort of exchange in which God always takes the full initiative but, in a certain sense, as we have seen on other occasions, he also needs Mary, her "yes" as a creature, her very flesh, her actual existence,

92

in order to prepare the matter for his sacrifice: the Body and the Blood, to offer them on the Cross as a means of eternal life and, in the Sacrament of the Eucharist, as spiritual food and drink.

Dear brothers and sisters, what happened in Mary also applies in ways that are different yet real to every man and to every woman because God asks each one of us to welcome him, to put at his disposal our heart and our body, our entire existence, our flesh the Bible says so that he may dwell in the world. He calls us to be united with him in the Sacrament of the Eucharist, Bread broken for the life of the world, to form together the Church, his Body in history. And if we say "yes", like Mary, indeed to the extent of our "yes", this mysterious exchange is also brought about for us and in us. We are taken up into the divinity of the One who took on our humanity. The Eucharist is the means, the instrument of this reciprocal transformation which always has God as its goal, and as the main actor. He is the Head and we are the limbs, he is the Vine and we the branches. Whoever eats of this Bread and lives in communion with Jesus, letting himself be transformed by him and in him, is saved from eternal death: naturally he dies like everyone and also shares in the mystery of Christ's Passion and Crucifixion, but he is no longer a slave to death and will rise on the Last Day to enjoy the eternal celebration together with Mary and with all the Saints.

This mystery, this celebration of God, begins here below: it is the mystery of faith, hope and love that is celebrated in life and in the liturgy, especially that of the Eucharist, and is expressed in fraternal communion and in service for our neighbour. Let us pray the Blessed Virgin to help us always to nourish ourselves faithfully with the Bread of eternal life, so that, already on this earth, we may experience the joy of Heaven.

From the

ANGELUS

*Courtyard of the Papal Summer Residence,
Castel Gandolfo
Sunday, 23 August 2009*

'You are the Holy One of God'

You know that for several Sundays the Liturgy has proposed for our reflection Chapter Six of John's Gospel, in which Jesus presents himself as the "Bread of life . . . which came down from Heaven", and, he adds: "if anyone eats of this bread, he will live for ever: and the bread which I shall give for the life of the world is my flesh" (Jn 6: 51). To the Jews who were arguing heatedly among themselves, questioning: "How can this man give us his flesh to eat?" (v. 52), and the world still debates it, Jesus replies in every age: "unless you eat the flesh of the Son of man and drink his blood, you have no life in you" (v. 53). We too should reflect on whether we have really understood this message. Today, the 21st Sunday of Ordinary Time, let us meditate on the last part of this chapter in which the Fourth Evangelist mentions the reaction of the people and of the disciples themselves. They were shocked by the Lord's words to the point that, having followed him until then, they exclaimed: "This is a hard saying; who can listen to it?" (v. 60). After this, "many of his disciples drew back and no longer went about with him" (v. 66) and the same thing has happened over and over again in various periods of history. One might expect Jesus to seek compromises to make himself better understood, but he does not mitigate what he says. On the contrary, he turns directly to the Twelve and asks them:

"Will you also go away?" (v. 67).

This provocative question is not only addressed to listeners in his time, but also reaches the believers and people of every epoch. Today too, many are "shocked" by the paradox of the Christian faith. Jesus' teaching seems "hard", too difficult to accept and to put into practice. Then there are those who reject it and abandon Christ; there are those who seek to "adapt" his word to the fashions of the times, misrepresenting its meaning and value. "Will you also go away?" This disturbing provocation resounds in our hearts and expects a personal answer from each one; it is a question addressed to each one of us. Jesus is not content with superficial and formal belonging, a first and enthusiastic adherence is not enough for him; on the contrary, what is necessary is to take part for one's whole life "in his thinking and in his willing". Following him fills our hearts with joy and gives full meaning to our existence, but it entails difficulties and sacrifices because very often we must swim against the tide.

"Will you also go away?" Peter answers Jesus' question on the Apostles' behalf, and in the name of believers of every century: "Lord, to whom shall we go? You have the words of eternal life; and we have believed, and have come to know, that you are the Holy One of God" (vv. 68-69).

Dear Brothers and Sisters, at this moment we too can and want to repeat Peter's answer, aware of course of our human frailty, of our problems and difficulties, but trusting in the power of the Holy Spirit which is expressed and manifested in communion with Jesus. Faith is a gift of God to man and at the same time man's free and total entrustment to God; faith is docile listening to the word of the Lord who is the "lamp" for our feet and a "light" for our path (cf. Ps 119 [118]: 105). If we open our hearts to Christ with trust, if we let ourselves be won over by him, we can also experience, like, for example, the holy Curé d'Ars, that "our only happiness on this earth is to love God and to know that he loves us." Let us ask the Virgin Mary always to keep awake within us this faith imbued with love, which made her, a humble girl of Nazareth, the Mother of God and Mother and model of all.

III

SACRAMENTUM CARITATIS

From the

POST-SYNODAL APOSTOLIC EXHORTATION SACRAMENTUM CARITATIS

To the bishops, clergy,
consecrated persons
and the lay faithful
on the eucharist
as the source and summit
of the church's life and mission

Given in Rome, at Saint Peter's,
on 22 February, the Feast of the Chair of Peter, 2007*

INTRODUCTION

1. The sacrament of charity (1), the Holy Eucharist is the gift that Jesus Christ makes of himself, thus revealing to us God's infinite love for every man and woman. This wondrous sacrament makes manifest that "greater" love which led him to "lay down his life for his friends" (Jn 15: 13). Jesus did indeed love them "to the end" (Jn 13: 1). In those words the Evangelist introduces Christ's act of immense humility: before dying for us on the Cross, he tied a towel around himself and washed the feet of his disciples. In the same way, Jesus continues, in the sacrament

---

* The original paragraph numbers and the numbering of endnotes have been retained for ease of cross-referencing with the whole document.

of the Eucharist, to love us "to the end", even to offering us his Body and his Blood. What amazement must the Apostles have felt in witnessing what the Lord did and said during that Supper! What wonder must the eucharistic mystery also awaken in our own hearts!

The food of truth

2. In the Sacrament of the altar, the Lord meets us, men and women created in God's image and likeness (cf. Gen 1: 27), and becomes our companion along the way. In this sacrament, the Lord truly becomes food for us, to satisfy our hunger for truth and freedom. Since only the truth can make us free (cf. Jn 8: 32), Christ becomes for us the food of truth. With deep human insight, Saint Augustine clearly showed how we are moved spontaneously, and not by constraint, whenever we encounter something attractive and desirable. Asking himself what it is that can move us most deeply, the saintly bishop went on to say: "What does our soul desire more passionately than truth?" (2) Each of us has an innate and irrepressible desire for ultimate and definitive truth. The Lord Jesus, "the way, and the truth, and the life" (Jn 14: 6), speaks to our thirsting, pilgrim hearts, our hearts yearning for the source of life, our hearts longing for truth. Jesus Christ is the Truth in person, drawing the world to himself. "Jesus is the lodestar of human freedom: without him, freedom loses its focus, for without the knowledge of truth, freedom becomes debased, alienated and reduced to empty caprice. With him, freedom finds itself." (3) In the Sacrament of the Eucharist, Jesus shows us in particular the *truth about the love* which is the very essence of God. It is this evangelical truth which challenges each of us and our whole being. For this reason, the Church, which finds in the Eucharist the very centre of her life, is constantly concerned to proclaim to all, in season and out of season (cf. 2 Tim 4: 2), that God is love. (4) Precisely because Christ has become for us the food of truth,

the Church turns to every man and woman, inviting them freely to accept God's gift.

The Church's eucharistic faith

6. *"The mystery of faith!"* With these words, spoken immediately after the words of consecration, the priest proclaims the mystery being celebrated and expresses his wonder before the substantial change of bread and wine into the Body and Blood of the Lord Jesus, a reality which surpasses all human understanding. The Eucharist is a "mystery of faith" par excellence: "the sum and summary of our faith." (13) The Church's faith is essentially a eucharistic faith, and it is especially nourished at the table of the Eucharist. Faith and the sacraments are two complementary aspects of ecclesial life. Awakened by the preaching of God's word, faith is nourished and grows in the grace-filled encounter with the Risen Lord which takes place in the sacraments: "faith is expressed in the rite, while the rite reinforces and strengthens faith." (14) For this reason, the Sacrament of the Altar is always at the heart of the Church's life: "thanks to the Eucharist, the Church is reborn ever anew!" (15) The more lively the eucharistic faith of the People of God, the deeper is its sharing in ecclesial life in steadfast commitment to the mission entrusted by Christ to his disciples. The Church's very history bears witness to this. Every great reform has in some way been linked to the rediscovery of belief in the Lord's eucharistic presence among his people.

The Bread come down from heaven

7. The first element of eucharistic faith is the mystery of God himself, trinitarian love. In Jesus' dialogue with Nicodemus, we find an illuminating expression in this regard: "God so loved the world that he gave his only Son, that whoever believes in him should not perish but have eternal life. For God sent the Son into the world, not to condemn the world, but that the world

might be saved through him" (Jn 3: 16-17). These words show the deepest source of God's gift. In the Eucharist Jesus does not give us a "thing", but himself; he offers his own Body and pours out his own Blood. He thus gives us the totality of his life and reveals the ultimate origin of this love. He is the eternal Son, given to us by the Father. In the Gospel we hear how Jesus, after feeding the crowds by multiplying the loaves and fishes, says to those who had followed him to the synagogue of Capernaum: "My Father gives you the true bread from heaven; for the bread of God is he who comes down from heaven, and gives life to the world" (Jn 6: 32-33), and even identifies himself, his own flesh and blood, with that bread: "I am the living bread which came down from heaven; if anyone eats of this bread, he will live forever; and the bread which I shall give for the life of the world is my flesh" (Jn 6: 51). Jesus thus shows that he is the bread of life which the eternal Father gives to mankind.

The new and eternal covenant in the blood of the Lamb

9. The mission for which Jesus came among us was accomplished in the Paschal Mystery. On the Cross from which he draws all people to himself (cf. Jn 12: 32), just before "giving up the Spirit", he utters the words: "it is finished" (Jn 19: 30). In the mystery of Christ's obedience unto death, even death on a Cross (cf. Phil 2: 8), the new and eternal covenant was brought about. In his crucified flesh, God's freedom and our human freedom met definitively in an inviolable, eternally valid pact. Human sin was also redeemed once for all by God's Son (cf. Heb 7: 27; 1 Jn 2: 2, 4: 10). As I have said elsewhere, "Christ's death on the Cross is the culmination of that turning of God against himself in which he gives himself in order to raise man up and save him. This is love in its most radical form." (18) In the Paschal Mystery, our deliverance from evil and death has taken place. In instituting the Eucharist, Jesus had spoken of the "new and eternal covenant"

in the shedding of his blood (cf. Mt 26: 28; Mk 14: 24; Lk 22: 20). This, the ultimate purpose of his mission, was clear from the very beginning of his public life. Indeed, when, on the banks of the Jordan, John the Baptist saw Jesus coming towards him, he cried out: "Behold, the Lamb of God, who takes away the sin of the world" (Jn 1: 29). It is significant that these same words are repeated at every celebration of Holy Mass, when the priest invites us to approach the altar: "This is *the Lamb of God* who takes away the sins of the world. Happy are those who are called to his supper." Jesus is the *true* paschal lamb who freely gave himself in sacrifice for us, and thus brought about the new and eternal covenant. The Eucharist contains this radical newness, which is offered to us again at every celebration. (19)

The institution of the Eucharist

10. This leads us to reflect on the institution of the Eucharist at the Last Supper. It took place within a ritual meal commemorating the foundational event of the people of Israel: their deliverance from slavery in Egypt. This ritual meal, which called for the sacrifice of lambs (cf. Ex 12: 1-28, 43-51), was a remembrance of the past, but at the same time a prophetic remembrance, the proclamation of a deliverance yet to come. The people had come to realize that their earlier liberation was not definitive, for their history continued to be marked by slavery and sin. The remembrance of their ancient liberation thus expanded to the invocation and expectation of a yet more profound, radical, universal and definitive salvation. This is the context in which Jesus introduces the newness of his gift. In the prayer of praise, the *Berakah*, he does not simply thank the Father for the great events of past history, but also for his own "exaltation". In instituting the Sacrament of the Eucharist, Jesus anticipates and makes present the sacrifice of the Cross and the victory of the Resurrection. At the same time, he reveals that he himself is

the *true* sacrificial lamb, destined in the Father's plan from the foundation of the world, as we read in The First Letter of Peter (cf. 1: 18-20). By placing his gift in this context, Jesus shows the salvific meaning of his death and Resurrection, a mystery which renews history and the whole cosmos. The institution of the Eucharist demonstrates how Jesus' death, for all its violence and absurdity, became in him a supreme act of love and mankind's definitive deliverance from evil.

Figura transit in veritatem

11. Jesus thus brings his own radical *novum* to the ancient Hebrew sacrificial meal. For us Christians, that meal no longer need be repeated. As the Church Fathers rightly say, *figura transit in veritatem*: the foreshadowing has given way to the truth itself. The ancient rite has been brought to fulfilment and definitively surpassed by the loving gift of the incarnate Son of God. The food of truth, Christ sacrificed for our sake, *dat figuris terminum*. (20) By his command to "do this in remembrance of me" (Lk 22: 19; 1 Cor 11:25), he asks us to respond to his gift and to make it sacramentally present. In these words the Lord expresses, as it were, his expectation that the Church, born of his sacrifice, will receive this gift, developing under the guidance of the Holy Spirit the liturgical form of the Sacrament. The remembrance of his perfect gift consists not in the mere repetition of the Last Supper, but in the Eucharist itself, that is, in the radical newness of Christian worship. In this way, Jesus left us the task of entering into his "hour". "The Eucharist draws us into Jesus' act of self-oblation. More than just statically receiving the incarnate *Logos*, we enter into the very dynamic of his self-giving." (21) Jesus "draws us into himself." (22) The substantial conversion of bread and wine into his Body and Blood introduces within creation the principle of a radical change, a sort of "nuclear fission", to use an image familiar to us today, which penetrates to the heart of all being, a change

meant to set off a process which transforms reality, a process leading ultimately to the transfiguration of the entire world, to the point where God will be all in all (cf. 1 Cor 15:28).

The Holy Spirit and the eucharistic celebration

13. An awareness of [the decisive role played by the Holy Spirit] is clearly evident in the Fathers of the Church. Saint Cyril of Jerusalem, in his *Catecheses*, states that we "call upon God in his mercy to send his Holy Spirit upon the offerings before us, to transform the bread into the body of Christ and the wine into the blood of Christ. Whatever the Holy Spirit touches is sanctified and completely transformed" (25). Saint John Chrysostom too notes that the priest invokes the Holy Spirit when he celebrates the sacrifice: (26) like Elijah, the minister calls down the Holy Spirit so that "as grace comes down upon the victim, the souls of all are thereby inflamed" (27). The spiritual life of the faithful can benefit greatly from a better appreciation of the richness of the anaphora: along with the words spoken by Christ at the Last Supper, it contains the epiclesis, the petition to the Father to send down the gift of the Spirit so that the bread and the wine will become the Body and Blood of Jesus Christ and that "the community as a whole will become ever more the body of Christ" (28). The Spirit invoked by the celebrant upon the gifts of bread and wine placed on the altar is the same Spirit who gathers the faithful "into one body" and makes of them a spiritual offering pleasing to the Father (29).

The Eucharist, causal principle of the Church

14. Through the Sacrament of the Eucharist Jesus draws the faithful into his "hour"; he shows us the bond that he willed to establish between himself and us, between his own person and the Church. Indeed, in the sacrifice of the Cross, Christ gave birth to the Church as his Bride and his Body. The Fathers of

the Church often meditated on the relationship between Eve's coming forth from the side of Adam as he slept (cf. Gen 2: 21-23) and the coming forth of the new Eve, the Church, from the open side of Christ sleeping in death: from Christ's pierced side, John recounts, there came forth blood and water (cf. Jn 19: 34), the symbol of the sacraments (30). A contemplative gaze "upon him whom they have pierced" (Jn 19: 37) leads us to reflect on the causal connection between Christ's sacrifice, the Eucharist and the Church. The Church "draws her life from the Eucharist" (31). Since the Eucharist makes present Christ's redeeming sacrifice, we must start by acknowledging that "there is a causal influence of the Eucharist at the Church's very origins" (32). The Eucharist is Christ who gives himself to us and continually builds us up as his Body. Hence, in the striking interplay between the Eucharist which builds up the Church, and the Church herself which "makes" the Eucharist (33), the primary causality is expressed in the first formula: the Church is able to celebrate and adore the mystery of Christ present in the Eucharist precisely because Christ first gave himself to her in the sacrifice of the Cross. The Church's ability to "make" the Eucharist is completely rooted in Christ's self-gift to her. Here we can see more clearly the meaning of Saint John's words: "he first loved us" (1 Jn 4:19). We too, at every celebration of the Eucharist, confess the primacy of Christ's gift. The causal influence of the Eucharist at the Church's origins definitively discloses both the chronological and ontological priority of the fact that it was Christ who loved us "first". For all eternity he remains the one who loves us first.

The Eucharist: a gift to men and women on their journey

30. If it is true that the sacraments are part of the Church's pilgrimage through history (99) towards the full manifestation of the victory of the risen Christ, it is also true that, especially

in the liturgy of the Eucharist, they give us a real foretaste of the eschatological fulfilment for which every human being and all creation are destined (cf. Rom 8: 19ff.). Man is created for that true and eternal happiness which only God's love can give. But our wounded freedom would go astray were it not already able to experience something of that future fulfilment. Moreover, to move forward in the right direction, we all need to be guided towards our final goal. That goal is Christ himself, the Lord who conquered sin and death, and who makes himself present to us in a special way in the eucharistic celebration. Even though we remain "aliens and exiles" in this world (1 Pet 2: 11), through faith we already share in the fullness of risen life. The eucharistic banquet, by disclosing its powerful eschatological dimension, comes to the aid of our freedom as we continue our journey.

The eschatological banquet

31. Reflecting on this mystery, we can say that Jesus' coming responded to an expectation present in the people of Israel, in the whole of humanity and ultimately in creation itself. By his self-gift, he objectively inaugurated the eschatological age. Christ came to gather together the scattered People of God (cf. Jn 11: 52) and clearly manifested his intention to gather together the community of the covenant, in order to bring to fulfilment the promises made by God to the fathers of old (cf. Jer 23: 3; Lk 1:55, 70). In the calling of the Twelve, which is to be understood in relation to the twelve tribes of Israel, and in the command he gave them at the Last Supper, before his redemptive passion, to celebrate his memorial, Jesus showed that he wished to transfer to the entire community which he had founded the task of being, within history, the sign and instrument of the eschatological gathering that had its origin in him. Consequently, every eucharistic celebration sacramentally accomplishes the eschatological gathering of the People of God. For us, the eucharistic banquet is a real foretaste of the final banquet

foretold by the prophets (cf. Is 25: 6-9) and described in the New Testament as "the marriage-feast of the Lamb" (Rev 19: 7-9), to be celebrated in the joy of the communion of saints (100).

The Church's social teaching

91. The mystery of the Eucharist inspires and impels us to work courageously within our world to bring about that renewal of relationships which has its inexhaustible source in God's gift. The prayer which we repeat at every Mass: "Give us this day our daily bread," obliges us to do everything possible, in cooperation with international, state and private institutions, to end or at least reduce the scandal of hunger and malnutrition afflicting so many millions of people in our world, especially in developing countries. In a particular way, the Christian laity, formed at the school of the Eucharist, are called to assume their specific political and social responsibilities. To do so, they need to be adequately prepared through practical education in charity and justice. To this end, the Synod considered it necessary for dioceses and Christian communities to teach and promote the Church's social doctrine. (248) In this precious legacy handed down from the earliest ecclesial tradition, we find elements of great wisdom that guide Christians in their involvement in today's burning social issues. This teaching, the fruit of the Church's whole history, is distinguished by realism and moderation; it can help to avoid misguided compromises or false utopias.

Conclusion

94. Dear brothers and sisters, the Eucharist is at the root of every form of holiness, and each of us is called to the fullness of life in the Holy Spirit. How many saints have advanced along the way of perfection thanks to their eucharistic devotion! From Saint Ignatius of Antioch to Saint Augustine, from Saint Anthony the Abbot to Saint Benedict, from Saint Francis of Assisi to Saint Thomas Aquinas,

from Saint Clare of Assisi to Saint Catherine of Siena, from Saint Paschal Baylon to Saint Peter Julian Eymard, from Saint Alphonsus Liguori to Blessed Charles de Foucauld, from Saint John Mary Vianney to Saint Thérèse of Lisieux, from Saint Pio of Pietrelcina to Blessed Teresa of Calcutta, from Blessed Piergiorgio Frassati to Blessed Ivan Merz, to name only a few, holiness has always found its centre in the Sacrament of the Eucharist.

This most holy mystery thus needs to be firmly believed, devoutly celebrated and intensely lived in the Church. Jesus' gift of himself in the Sacrament which is the memorial of his passion tells us that the success of our lives is found in our participation in the trinitarian life offered to us truly and definitively in him. The celebration and worship of the Eucharist enable us to draw near to God's love and to persevere in that love until we are united with the Lord whom we love. The offering of our lives, our fellowship with the whole community of believers and our solidarity with all men and women are essential aspects of that *logiké latreía*, spiritual worship, holy and pleasing to God (cf. Rom 12: 1), which transforms every aspect of our human existence, to the glory of God. I therefore ask all pastors to spare no effort in promoting an authentically eucharistic Christian spirituality. Priests, deacons and all those who carry out a eucharistic ministry should always be able to find in this service, exercised with care and constant preparation, the strength and inspiration needed for their personal and communal path of sanctification. I exhort the lay faithful, and families in particular, to find ever anew in the Sacrament of Christ's love the energy needed to make their lives an authentic sign of the presence of the risen Lord. I ask all consecrated men and women to show by their eucharistic lives the splendour and the beauty of belonging totally to the Lord.

95. At the beginning of the fourth century, Christian worship was still forbidden by the imperial authorities. Some Christians in North Africa, who felt bound to celebrate the Lord's Day,

defied the prohibition. They were martyred after declaring that it was not possible for them to live without the Eucharist, the food of the Lord: *sine dominico non possumus*. (252) May these martyrs of Abitinae, in union with all those saints and beati who made the Eucharist the centre of their lives, intercede for us and teach us to be faithful to our encounter with the risen Christ. We too cannot live without partaking of the Sacrament of our salvation; we too desire to be *iuxta dominicam viventes*, to reflect in our lives what we celebrate on the Lord's Day. That day is the day of our definitive deliverance. Is it surprising, then, that we should wish to live every day in that newness of life which Christ has brought us in the mystery of the Eucharist?

96. May Mary Most Holy, the Immaculate Virgin, ark of the new and eternal covenant, accompany us on our way to meet the Lord who comes. In her we find realized most perfectly the essence of the Church. The Church sees in Mary – "Woman of the Eucharist", as she was called by the Servant of God John Paul II (253) – her finest icon, and she contemplates Mary as a singular model of the eucharistic life. For this reason, as the priest prepares to receive on the altar the *verum Corpus natum de Maria Virgine*, speaking on behalf of the liturgical assembly, he says in the words of the canon: "We honour Mary, the ever-virgin mother of Jesus Christ our Lord and God" (254). Her holy name is also invoked and venerated in the canons of the Eastern Christian traditions. The faithful, for their part, "commend to Mary, Mother of the Church, their lives and the work of their hands. Striving to have the same sentiments as Mary, they help the whole community to become a living offering pleasing to the Father" (255). She is the *tota pulchra*, the all-beautiful, for in her the radiance of God's glory shines forth. The beauty of the heavenly liturgy, which must be reflected in our own assemblies, is faithfully mirrored in her. From Mary we must learn to become men and women of the Eucharist and of the Church,

and thus to present ourselves, in the words of Saint Paul, "holy and blameless" before the Lord, even as he wished us to be from the beginning (cf. Col 1: 22; Eph 1: 4) (256).

97. Through the intercession of the Blessed Virgin Mary, may the Holy Spirit kindle within us the same ardour experienced by the disciples on the way to Emmaus (cf. Lk 24: 13-35) and renew our "eucharistic wonder" through the splendour and beauty radiating from the liturgical rite, the efficacious sign of the infinite beauty of the holy mystery of God. Those disciples arose and returned in haste to Jerusalem in order to share their joy with their brothers and sisters in the faith. True joy is found in recognizing that the Lord is still with us, our faithful companion along the way. The Eucharist makes us discover that Christ, risen from the dead, is our contemporary in the mystery of the Church, his Body. Of this mystery of love we have become witnesses. Let us encourage one another to walk joyfully, our hearts filled with wonder, towards our encounter with the Holy Eucharist, so that we may experience and proclaim to others the truth of the words with which Jesus took leave of his disciples: "Lo, I am with you always, until the end of the world" (Mt 28: 20).

(1) Cf. Saint Thomas Aquinas, *Summa Theologiae* III, q. 73, a. 3.

(2) Saint Augustine, *In Iohannis Evangelium Tractatus*, 26,5: PL 35, 1609.

(3) Benedict XVI, Address to Participants in the Plenary Assembly of the Congregation for the Doctrine of the Faith (10 February 2006): AAS 98 (2006), 255.

(4) Benedict XVI, Address to the Members of the Ordinary Council of the General Secretariat of the Synod of Bishops (1 June 2006): *L'Osservatore Romano*, 2 June 2006, p. 5.

(13) *Catechism of the Catholic Church*, 1327.

(14) *Propositio* 16.

(15) Benedict XVI, Homily at the Mass of Installation in the Cathedral of Rome (7 May 2005): AAS 97 (2005), 752.

(18) Encyclical Letter *Deus Caritas Est* (25 December 2005), 12: AAS 98 (2006), 228.

(19) Cf. *Propositio* 3.

(20) Roman Breviary, Hymn for the Office of Readings of the Solemnity of Corpus Christi.

(21) Benedict XVI, Encyclical Letter *Deus Caritas Est* (25 December 2005), 13: AAS 98 (2006), 228.

(22) Benedict XVI, Homily at Marienfeld Esplanade (21 August 2005): AAS 97 (2005), 891-892.

(25) *Cat.* XXIII, 7: PG 33, 1114ff.

(26) Cf. *De Sacerdotio*, VI, 4: PG 48, 681.

(27) Ibid., III, 4: PG 48, 642.

(28) *Propositio* 22.

(29) Cf. *Propositio* 42: "This eucharistic encounter takes place in the Holy Spirit, who transforms and sanctifies us. He re-awakens in the disciple the firm desire to proclaim boldly to others all that he has heard and experienced, to bring them to the same encounter with Christ. Thus the disciple, sent forth by the Church, becomes open to a mission without frontiers."

(30) Cf. Second Vatican Ecumenical Council, Dogmatic Constitution on the Church *Lumen Gentium*, 3; for an example, see: Saint John Chrysostom, *Catechesis* 3, 13-19: SC 50, 174-177.

(31) John Paul II, Encyclical Letter *Ecclesia de Eucharistia* (17 April 2003), 1: AAS 95 (2003), 433.

(32) Ibid., 21: AAS 95 (2003), 447.

(33) Cf. John Paul II, Encyclical Letter *Redemptor Hominis* (4 March 1979), 20: AAS 71 (1979), 309-316; Apostolic Letter *Dominicae Cenae* (24 February 1980), 4: AAS 72 (1980), 119-121.

(99) Cf. Second Vatican Ecumenical Council, Dogmatic Constitution on the Church *Lumen Gentium*, 48.

(100) Cf. *Propositio* 3.

(248) Cf. *Propositio* 48. In this regard, the *Compendium of the Social Doctrine of the Church* has proved most helpful.

(252) *Martyrium Saturnini, Dativi et aliorum plurimorum*, 7, 9, 10: PL 8, 707, 709-710.

(253) Cf. John Paul II, Encyclical Letter *Ecclesia de Eucharistia* (17 April 2003), 53: AAS 95 (2003), 469.

(254) Eucharistic Prayer I (Roman Canon).

(255) *Propositio* 50.

(256) Cf. Benedict XVI, Homily (8 December 2005): AAS 98 (2006), 15.

Also from Family Publications

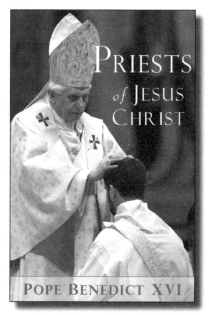

Priests of Jesus Christ

Pope Benedict XVI

In this book, the Holy Father combines insight with clarity as he elucidates different aspects of the priestly vocation and the theology of the priesthood, and shows how the life and ministry of the priest are centred on Christ. This book is therefore invaluable not only for priests, deacons and seminarians, but also for members of the laity to understand the mission of their priest and the role he plays in the Church.

His words will inspire priests, seminarians, those discerning God's calling and all members of the Church, above all to give thanks to God for the gift of priests in the mystery of Jesus Christ.

Paperback   272 pages   **£12.95**